BUILD WEBSITES THAT WORK WITH ADOBE DREAMWEAVER CS5

Marek Mularczyk

www.SaiTraining.co.uk

Build websites that work with Adobe Dreamweaver CS5

Published by Sai Training

ISBN - 978-0-9571214-0-9 (Paperback)
ISBN - 978-0-9571214-1-6 (PDF)

www.saitraining.co.uk
www.marekmularczyk.com

For my beloved daughter Julia
who passed away as I was finishing this book...

I will always love you.

Table of Contents

6

Introduction

Dreamweaver is an industry standard in web authoring. Dreamweaver offers tools for quick and easy design of web pages. And Dreamweaver is a professional tool that professional web designers, as well as web enthusiasts, use on daily basis.

This book was designed so that you could follow at your own pace. Every new lessons introduces a new concept and builds on what you have learnt in previous lessons. If you have used Dreamweaver a bit, or if you haven't used it before, you will see how easy it is to learn Dreamweaver. If you have been using Dreamweaver for some time, you will learn some new features and techniques to give you cutting edge in Dreamweaver CS5.

You can learn the way you like it. You can follow the lessons step by step, or you can jump to the lesson you are interested in. Each lesson gives you clear instructions and easy to follow steps.

Before you start

Before you start, you need to have knowledge of using your computer/your operating system - Dreamweaver works in the same way on both Windows and Mac. You do not need to have knowledge of Dreamweaver , the book was created for beginners as well as more advanced users. You just need to know how to operate your computer, mouse, menus in Dreamweaver, and how to Open and Save the files.

Installing Dreamweaver

Before you start, you need to install Dreamweaver. You can purchase Dreamweaver straight from Adobe at http://www.adobe.com or from one of the Adobe resellers. Dreamweaver can also be downloaded as a 30-day trial, so you can try it out before you purchase it.

Dreamweaver can be purchased as a stand-alone application or as part of one of the Creative Suite editions . For more information go to Adobe web-site at http://www.adobe.com.

Working with the lessons

Each lesson comes with files that you can use to follow along.
If you want to use them you need to copy them onto your computer to your preferred location. You can copy the files to any folder anywhere on your computer, I use Desktop as an example but free to copy them to any location you like.
The files can be downloaded from the following address:
http://saitraining.co.uk/books/dwcs5.zip.

Keep Dreamweaver updated

To get the best out of Dreamweaver keep it updated. Adobe releases software updates every now and then. All the updates are free so why not use them? Here's how you can get the updates for Dreamweaver:

- In Dreamweaver choose Help > Updates. Adobe Updater will open and check if there are any available updates.
- If there are any updates you want to install, select them and click Download and Install updates.

This will install the updates for you. The installation process is very easy.

Lesson 1

Introducing Dreamweaver CS5

In this lesson you're going to familiarize yourself with Dreamweaver CS5 and learn how to:

- Explore Dreamweaver interface

- Work with panels

- Use Welcome Screen

- Create, open and save documents

- Learn how websites work

You will also learn what's new in Dreamweaver CS5.

This lesson will take about 45 minutes to complete.

Why Adobe Dreamweaver CS5?

Adobe Dreamweaver is the industry leading HTML (Hypertext Markup Language) editor. Its popularity has many reasons. It offers an incredible set of coding and developing tools for new and experienced users alike. Dreamweaver offers something for all users:

- designers love What You See Is What You Get (WYSIWYG) functionality as they add content, which saves them hours of work trying to preview the pages with a web browser. It is so easy to use that novices will appreciate how quickly and easily content can be added to the pages using its simple to use interface.
- coders love all the enhancements built into the Code View inside Dreamweaver, with support for PHP, ASP, ColdFusion, and JavaScript.

Dreamweaver's popularity comes from its simplicity in taking the site from a concept stage to the launch of the website, all within Dreamweaver with its built-in ftp functionality used to upload the website to the web server. This makes Dreamweaver a preferred tool with web designers and developers. At the same time, it is an easy and very intuitive tool, so even novices find it easy to use to build their own websites.

Explore Dreamweaver Interface

The Dreamweaver interface features many customisable panels and toolbars. It's amazing that such a powerful application, that offers so much within its interface, provides a huge number of options to minimize, hide and rearrange panels and toolbars.

This lesson will start with the Dreamweaver interface so you can understand how Dreamweaver works. If you want to follow along, choose File > Open. When the Open dialogue box appears, navigate to Lesson_01 folder and choose **start.html**. Click Open.

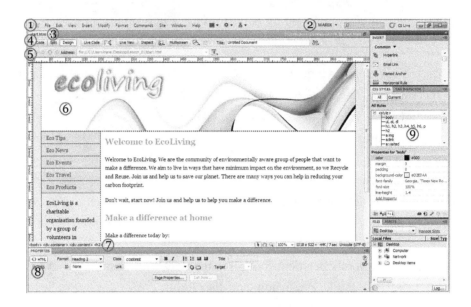

Dreamweaver's fully configurable interface. Familiarize yourself with the names of the components.

① Menu Bar   ⑥ Document in Design View

② Workspace Menu   ⑦ Tag Selectors

③ Document Title Bar   ⑧ Property Inspector

④ Document Toolbar   ⑨ Panels

⑤ Browser Navigation Toolbar

Dreamweaver's panels

Dreamweaver ships with many panels, that by default appear on the right side of the Dreamweaver interface. These panels make it easy to insert text, images, and media and much more. Insert panel, just for an for example, is used to insert content on the page, e.g. images, text etc and Dreamweaver will insert all the required code for you so you don't need to know anything about coding. All the commands found in the Insert panel, can also be found under the Insert menu.

If you look under the Window menu, any panel that is open will have a check mark next to its name. Sometimes, a panel may appear behind another panel on the screen (like Assets and AP Elements Panels on the screenshot below.

In this situation, simply select the desired panel in the Window menu and it will appear on the top of the stack.

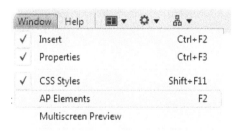

Working with panels

You can minimize or expand individual panels to create more space for some panels. If you want to minimize a panel, double click the tab containing the name of the panel. If you want to expand the panel, double click the tab containing the name of the panel again.

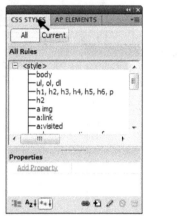 

Dreamweaver comes with a set of prebuilt workspaces and you can quickly use them. The workspaces have been created by experts to put the tools you need just where you need them.

Dreamweaver CS5 ships with eight workspaces to access them, choose one of them from the Workspace menu located at the top of the Dreamweaver interface.

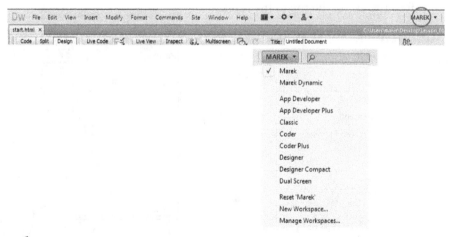

Here are a few examples of workspaces:

Classic Workspace

displays panels and toolbars the way they used to appear in older versions of Dreamweaver.

Designer Workspace

a perfect workspace for visual designers.

Coder Workspace

this workspace focuses on the coding environment and Dreamweaver's coding tools.

Design, Code and Split Views

Dreamweaver offers three ways to view your document: Design view, Code view and Split view. The Views Buttons can be found in the Document Toolbar as shown on the screenshot below.

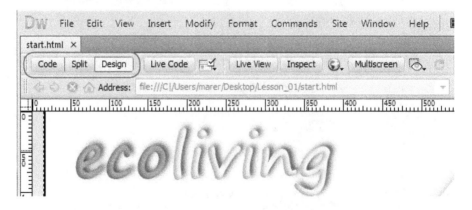

Design view

In Design view, Dreamweaver turns into a WYSIWYG editor, meaning it provides a close preview of the page the way it is going to look like in a web browser. It is a very close match to what you see in a web browser. To work in Design view, click on Design view button in Document toolbar.

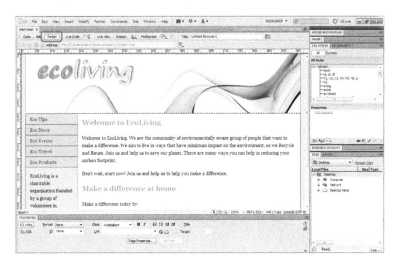

Code view

Code view focuses on working on HMTL code in Dreamweaver. It also displays a variety of coding tools to make your work easier. To start working in a Code view, click on Code view button in Document toolbar.

19

Split view

Split view provides a mix of both: Design and Code view at the same time. Changes made in one window update in the other at the same time. To start working in a Split view, click on Split view button in the Document toolbar.

While working in Split view, you can choose if you want to split it horizontally or vertically. To access this option, choose View > Split Vertically.

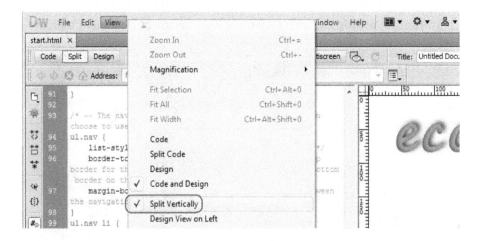

Welcome screen

The Welcome screen appears when you start Dreamweaver and every time you have no documents open. You can choose to hide the Welcome screen, and later on display it if you change your mind. If you hide the Welcome screen, the document window will be blank.

If you want to hide the Welcome screen, select Don't show again option on the Welcome screen (bottom left corner). I personally would encourage to leave it on as it gives you access to loads of very useful options.

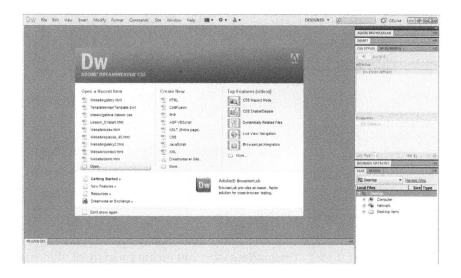

If you have hidden the Welcome screen and want to bring it back, select Edit > Preferences on Windows (Dreamweaver > Preferences on a Mac) and select the Show Welcome screen option.

If you are new to Dreamweaver, you will find the Welcome screen very useful. Let's have a look on what options the Welcome screen provides and how to use them effectively.

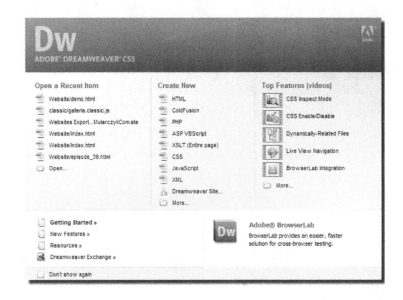

Let's start from left:

Open a Recent Item - a list of the recent files you worked on appears here, you can also browse to open a document by clicking on Open button at the bottom. Open...

Create New - you can create a variety of different documents such as HTML pages, CSS, JavaScript, and many more. This is your starting point if you want to create a blank HTML page or a new CSS stylesheet. You can also define a new Dreamweaver Site by clicking on Dreamweaver Site button at the bottom. Dreamweaver Site...

Top Features (videos) - these are links and by clicking one of these links you can watch videos hosted on Adobe website about some of the new features in Dreamweaver CS5.

22

Create, Open, and Save Documents

This is a technique you will be using through the whole course. Every lesson will require that you either create or open a file and then save it. Here's how you can achieve these tasks.

Create New Documents

Dreamweaver can create a variety of different files, including HTML, CSS, and JavaScript just to name a few.

You can use starter pages that come with Dreamweaver to quickly and easily create pages without worrying about creating layout from scratch or you can create blank pages and build the layout yourself.

To create a new blank document use the centre section of the Welcome screen. If you want to use starter pages to quickly start adding content instead of building a page from scratch, choose **File > New**.

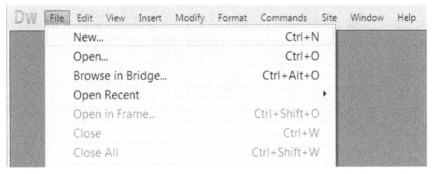

This will bring New Document dialogue box with many options, but we're going to focus on Blank Page section in the first column on the left as on the screenshot on the next page. In the New Document dialogue box, select Blank Page in the first column and HTML in the second column. This will give you access to all the starter pages that come with Dreamweaver.

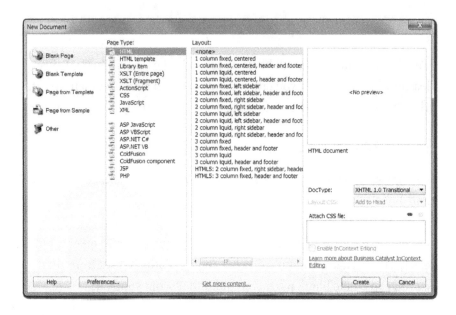

In the lessons to come, we will be using this dialogue box to create pages using the pre-designed CSS layouts that come with Dreamweaver. This is the easiest way to create modern pages with CSS layouts. A CSS page layout uses CSS (Cascading Style Sheets) format, instead of traditional HTML tables and frames, to position the content on the web page. More about CSS in the following lessons.

Dreamweaver comes with 16 CSS layouts plus 2 new layouts with HTML 5 specification. These layouts render properly in all versions of Firefox, Safari, Opera, Chrome and Internet Explorer 5.5 and later.

More about the CSS layouts later on. Now, let's have a quick look at how the websites work and then we're done with our first lesson so we could move on to the next one!

What's new in Dreamweaver CS5?

Dreamweaver CS5 brings many new features and enhancements to offer an integrated working environment in which web designers can design, test, and deploy their websites. Here are a few most important new features in Dreamweaver CS5:

Dynamically Related Files

If you plan to develop websites with web-based content management systems such as Wordpress or Joomla, the Dynamically Related Files feature in Dreamweaver CS5 will help you access the files and update your pages quickly.

Even a simple page in one of these systems has a number of files that need to load, and now Dreamweaver can discover these files for you with a single click.

Live View navigation

Live View navigation is an excellent new feature that expands on what Live View could do in Dreamweaver CS4 (Live View was introduced in Dreamweaver CS4). Using Live View navigation, you can view the page as it is being rendered in a standard compliant web browser, but you can also use links that are active and interact with a website. You will need to enable the Follow Links feature to navigate between the pages as on the screenshot below.

25

Enhanced CSS inspection

CSS is used to seperate the page content from the presentation. Because as a novice web designer you need to understand how the elements relate to one another, enhanced CSS tools in Dreamweaver CS5 give you more control in editing environment.

The Inspect Command
Now you can create CSS-based layouts more accurately with the ability to visually display the CSS box model with its properties (padding, margin etc) without installing third-party applications or using the code view. In Dreamweaver CS5, you can use the Inspect Command with the Live View to identify HTML elements and the CSS styles that they use.

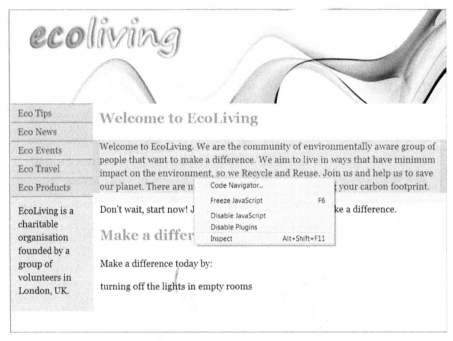

The colours around the text on the screenshot represent padding and margin.

CSS Enable/Disable

This is one of my favourites in Dreamweaver CS5. You can enable or disable a CSS property in the CSS Styles panel. When you disable a property, you're not really deleting it, it is just not rendered. This one feature enables you to keep working in the editing environment and by simply enabling/disabling the CSS property you can check how the changes affect your design.

Integration with Adobe BrowserLab

Dreamweaver CS5 integrates with BrowserLab, a service that is a part of new CS Live Services (CS Live Services are new in CS5). BrowserLab provides a fast and accurate solution for cross-browser testing. Using BrowserLab, you can preview your pages in multiple web browsers, and even in different versions and on different operating systems!

27

Enhanced CSS starter pages

Create quickly your pages with updated CSS starter layouts. CSS starter layouts are pre-designed pages that were created by a team of experts to help you quickly create pages with a layout in place and just start adding content.

The CSS starter pages have now been enhanced based on a feedback from users and a constant evolving of CSS so that Adobe could provide users with the latest up to date CSS starter pages. To give users a quick start, all the CSS starter pages in Dreamweaver CS5 have comments and instructions included in the code and within the page. CSS starter pages speed your designing time by providing many structures that you can use to start building pages.

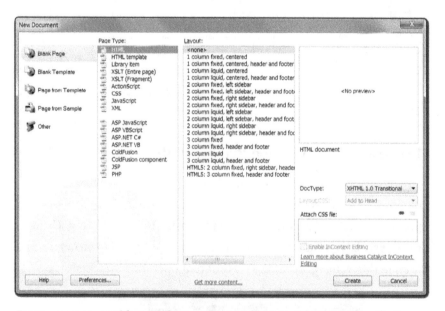

Dreamweaver comes with 16 CSS layouts plus 2 new layouts with HTML 5 specification. These layouts render properly in all versions of Firefox, Safari, Opera, Chrome and Internet Explorer 5.5 and later.

How websites work

Before you start building the web pages, let's look at some basics of how the websites work.

When you type in a web address, do you know what's happening? Most people don't. When you type a web address, you connect to a web server (a remote computer) and downloading all the required components of the page (images, documents). Your web browser is building the page for you based on the HTML code included in the web pages.

Just to clarify, there are a number of web browsers on the market and they're all free to download. The most popular ones are: Mozilla Firefox, Safari, Google Chrome, Opera, and Internet Explorer. Most of these web browsers work on both Windows and Mac, as well as on Linux.

When you build a page in Dreamweaver, all the HTML code is being built for you by Dreamweaver so you don't need to worry about how HTML works (although it helps to know some HTML, and we'll cover that in a chapter on HTML). You just work in Design view (or Split view), and Dreamweaver builds HTML code as you add text, images, and media.

Domain Names and Servers

When you type in a website address (such as *adobe.com*), you enter the website's domain name that was purchased by the website owner. The website is located on a web server.

A web server is just a machine like a computer with constant access to internet and with the ability to handle massive traffic from thousands of users. It needs constant access to internet so that your website is available 24 hours a day. Websites are usually hosted on web servers maintained by web hosting companies. These companies charge a fee to host your website, some big companies have their own servers.

29

There are a number of web hosting companies on the market, including well known brands like Yahoo and GoDaddy in the US. Depending on the country you reside in, you'll find lots of web hosting providers, just do a web search. The prices for web hosting usually start from around £3 a month ($5 a month).

Apart from paying for web hosting, you will also need to buy your domain name. You can buy your domain name from the same hosting company and this is a yearly or 2-yearly fee. Here are some examples of prices:

Per year pricing	1 year	2 years
.COM New	$11.99*	$11.99*
.CO New	$29.99 $11.99	$29.99 $20.99
.INFO New	$10.69* $1.99*	$10.69* $6.34*
.NET New	$14.99* $9.99*	$14.99* $12.49*
.ORG New	$11.99* $9.99*	$11.99* $12.49*
.ME New	$19.99 $8.99	$19.99 $14.49
.MOBI New	$17.99* $6.99*	$17.99* $12.49*
.US New	$19.99 $6.99	$19.99 $13.49
.BIZ New	$14.99* $5.99*	$14.99* $10.49*
.CA New	$12.99	$12.99
.CC New	$19.99	$19.99
.WS New	$14.99	$14.99
.ASIA New	$19.99* $8.99*	$19.99* $14.49*
.TV New	$39.99	$39.99

	TLDs	1 year	2 years
?	.com	FREE	$9.95
?	.net	FREE	$9.95
?	.org	FREE	$9.95
?	.we.bs	FREE	$4.50
?	.info	FREE	$9.95
?	.biz	FREE	$9.95
?	.us	FREE	$9.95

And we have finally arrived to the end of the lesson so it is time to move on to the next lesson so you can start working in Dreamweaver!

Let me leave you with some questions to revise what we've learned so far.

Review Questions

1. How can you show or hide any panel using the menu?

2. How do you switch between Code, Split, and Design views?

3. How can you create a new document that uses CSS starter pages?

4. Which workspace displays the panels the way they used to display in older versions of Dreamweaver?

Review Answers

1. All the panels in Dreamweaver are listed in the Window menu. To show or hide a panel, just select it from Window menu.

2. You can switch between Code, Split, and Design views using Code, Split, and Design view buttons located on the Document toolbar.

3. To create a new document that uses CSS starter pages, choose File > New, and then select Blank Page in the first column and HTML in the second column.

4. Classic Workspace displays panels and toolbars the way they used to appear in older versions of Dreamweaver

Lesson 2

HTML and CSS Basics

In this lesson you're going to familiarize yourself with HTML and CSS and learn how to:

- create HTML code using a Text editor

- understand how HTML syntax works

- create HTML with Dreamweaver

- differentiate HTML and CSS

- apply CSS formatting to the pages

This lesson will take about 1 hour 15 minutes to complete.

Why HTML and what is it?

HTML - Hypertext Markup Language - is what the web is based on. Just to clarify, HTML doesn't belong to anyone and the HTML pages can be created by many applications. You can create your HTML pages with any text editor because HTML pages are basically text files! The reason we're going to use Dreamweaver to create HTML pages is because Dreamweaver will do all the hard work creating code for you. If you ever need to edit your HTML page and you are away from your computer/don't have Dreamweaver, you could use text editor. It takes longer but you can do it.

Back to HTML, it is text based. Even though you don't need any HTML knowledge to create pages with Dreamweaver, it is good to have good understanding of how HTML works. HTML is used when inserting images or text on a page. Without HTML, the web browser wouldn't know how to display the content. Let's say you want to add some text to the page and you want to display it as a heading with a paragraph of text below. How does the web browser know which text is a heading and which one is a paragraph? You tell web browser how to display the text by using what we call "HTML Tags". Let's start by looking at the basic HTML code structure.

Basic HTML Structure

```
<html>
    <head>
        <title> My first web page. </title>
    </head>
        <body>
        <h1> Welcome to my first web page! </h1>
        </body>
</html>
```

35

Let me explain the code on the previous page. The properly structured HTML page contains HTML tags, most of which consist of opening and closing tags (there are some exceptions as usual but don't worry about that now). The opening tag consists of lesser than and greater than symbols with a tag inside, i.e.. **<html>**. The closing tag uses the same symbols and it also includes the backslash, i.e.. **</html>**.

Let's write some HTML code. Start by opening a text editor (any text editor will do except for Microsoft Word. Don't use Word as it adds too much unwanted code). If you're on Windows, you can use Notepad, on Mac you can use TextEdit.

Understanding HTML

1 Open Notepad (Windows) or TextEdit (Mac).

2 Type in the following code in the empty window:

```
<html>

<head>

</head>

<body>

<h1> Welcome to my first page! </h1>

</body>

</html>
```

3 Save the file as **mypage.html** using Save As command. In the dialogue box that opens choose **All Files** from the Save As type drop-down menu.

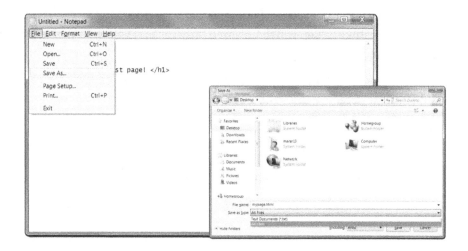

4 Open a web browser (Firefox, Safari or Explorer).

5 Choose File > Open. Navigate to the location where you saved the file

and select **mypage.html**. Click Open/OK.

Congratulations! You have just created your first web page and it didn't
even require a lot of coding.

Let me explain what happened here. The text that displays in a web browser is enclosed within h1 tag, which tells web browser that you want this text to be a big bold heading (h1 is the biggest heading in HTML, more on headings later on). Also, anything that appears between body tags appears on a page in the web browser.

Let's add one more line of code:

6 Below the line enclosed within h1 tag, add another line:

```
<p> This is the first paragraph below the main heading.
</p>
```

so now your code should read:

7 Save the file, open the web browser and preview the page. Here's what

you should see in a web browser.

This time, by adding a <p> tag, we let web browser know, that we wanted to display the text between the opening and closing <p> tag as a paragraph of text. As the web browser understands the HTML code, it displays the paragraph in its usual styling. In the later lessons, you will learn how using CSS you can change how the text displays in a web browser. You will also learn how easy and fun it is!

Let's make one more change to the code on the page. We'll try to add some space between the words *main* and *heading*, let's say we'll add five spaces between these words.

8 Navigate back to your text editor, and place your cursor in the code between the words *main* and *heading*. Press spacebar five times on your keyboard to add space. Notice how the space appears in the code.

9 Save the file.

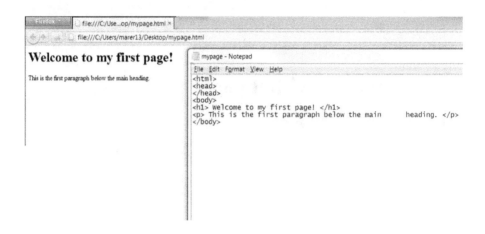

10 Navigate to your web browser and load the updated page.

As you can see, the web browser doesn't display the spaces between the words. It just ignores it, you could add loads of spaces here and they wouldn't display on the page. This is because the web browser ignores extra space. You can correct it by inserting an HTML tag, that a web browser will understand. Here's what you're going to do to add some extra space, that a web browser will understand.

11 Navigate back to your text editor

12 Put your cursor between the *main* and *heading* letters and add ** ** a few times. This piece of code adds nonbreaking space on a page.

13 Now your line with a paragraph in a text editor should look like that:

```
<p> This is the first paragraph below the main  
      heading. </p>
```

14 Save the file.

15 Navigate to your web browser and load the updated page.

Adding Meta Tags

Every web page consists of three main elements: html, head, and body, that create the structure of the page. Html element contains all the code for the page. This means all code appears between opening and closing tags. The body element contains all the content that will appear on the page within a web browser. The head element contains all the information for a web browser, i.e. web page title, description, and keywords - these three elements are also used by the search engines (google, yahoo, bing etc.). Add the title to your page first.

1 Open the page in your text editor (if you don't have it still open).

2 Add highlighted code before closing head tag like this:

```
<html>

<head>

<title> HTML Basics homepage. </title>

</head>
```

41

3 Save the page and test it in a web browser to see what's changed.

Did you notice any difference? You may not notice it at first, but when you look at your web browser's title bar, you'll notice your web page title.

The web browser displaying the web page title in the title bar of a web browser.

We will talk about the other head elements (keywords and description) a bit later on. Now you know how to create a simple page using just a text editor, so it is time for you to create the same page in Dreamweaver.

4 Close your text editor. You won't need it.

Creating HTML pages in Dreamweaver

Let's start with a very frequently asked question: "If I can create my pages with any text editor, why would I use Dreamweaver and spend all these money buying it, when I get a free text editor with my operating system?". You will see in the coming lessons, why Dreamweaver is so much better than text editors, because there are many reasons for that. But, you'll find out one reason right now. I don't want to keep you impatiently waiting.

In this exercise, we'll re-create the same page with Dreamweaver.

1 Launch Dreamweaver.

2 Choose HTML from the Create New column in the Welcome screen.

3 When new document opens, make sure you have Design view button

in the top left corner of the document window selected. Your page should

look like this:

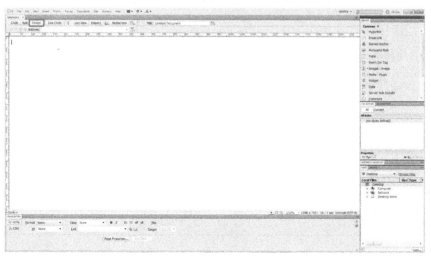

Dreamweaver displaying a new blank document in Design view.

43

4 Now switch to Code view by pressing the Code view button in the top left

corner of the document window and you should see quite a lot of code, that

was automatically generated by Dreamweaver. How clever?

Dreamweaver added a basic structure to your page even before you did
anything here. Html, head, and body tags are already here. You just need to
add the content and the title. That's what you're going to do now.

5 Select the Design view button to go back to Design view. You'll find it

easier to work in Design view and there is no need for working in Code view

right now.

6 The first element we added on the page was the heading on the top.

That's what you're going to add now. Click on the top of the page and you

should see a blinking cursor there. Just start typing the heading you added

previously.

The text initially appears as a paragraph text, so to change it into a heading navigate to the Properties panel at the bottom of the screen, click on the drop-down menu next to Format and select Heading 1.

Changing the text formatting using the Properties panel.

Here you go! Here's how easy it is to add a heading to your page. Next step will be to add a paragraph of text below.

Put your cursor at the end of the line and press Enter on your keyboard. This will move the cursor to a new line. Start typing to add a paragraph text.

Once you've added the text, put your cursor inside the paragraph and inspect what the Properties panel says. It should say Paragraph.

The Properties panel should say Paragraph because when you press Enter on your keyboard, Dreamweaver automatically creates a new paragraph of text.

10 Next step is to add a page title. Locate the Title field at the top of the document window, highlight "Untitled Document", and replace it with the title of the page - **HTML Basics homepage**, and press Enter.

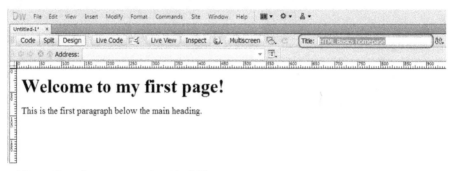

Adding a tile to the page using the Title field.

Using the Title field in Dreamweaver you managed to change the page title without going into the Code view and working with the HTML code.

11 Choose File > Save. Navigate to your desktop, and save it as **mypage2**.

You don't need to add the html file extension, Dreamweaver will do it for you automatically.

Dreamweaver adds the file extension automatically so you don't need to do it, but how do you know what file extension is Dreamweaver going to add? There is a whole list of file extensions, when you look under Save as type. Here's how to find out, what file extension Dreamweaver is going to use.

12 Navigate to your Dreamweaver Preferences by choosing Edit >

Preferences on Windows (Dreamweaver > Preferences on Mac). Choose

New Document category on the left. The default file extension for your

page can be found under Default extension.

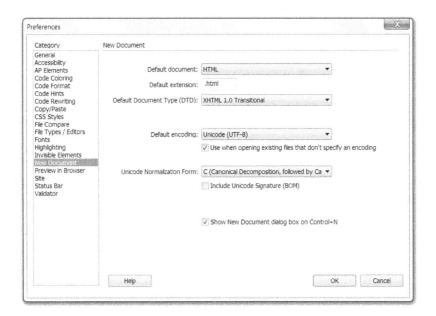

Now that you know, what file extension Dreamweaver uses, you can preview the page you created.

13 Choose File > Preview in Browser. The page you've created appears in a browser.

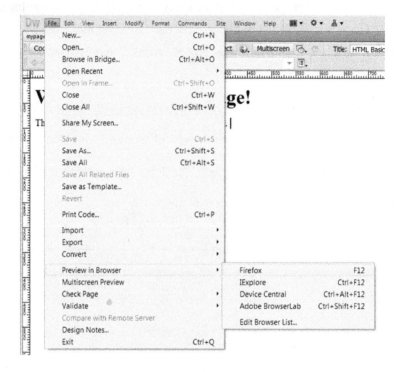

Now you can see, that you managed to create a page in Dreamweaver in a fraction of the time it took you to do it in a text editor.
Now it's time for some CSS basics.

Why CSS and what is it?

Do you know how the web pages were created in the past? Have you created one? In the past, to simulate a multicolumn layout web designers were using tables. However, HTML-based formatting using tables was quickly deprecated from the language, and the cascading style sheets (CSS) were introduced. CSS avoids all the problems we had designing HTML layouts. And it is much faster to change layout with CSS. Here's how we differentiate HTML from CSS. HTML is used to add content to your pages, while CSS is used to present the content, style it. So basically, HTML > Content, CSS > Presentation.

HTML vs. CSS - Formatting Pages

In this exercise, you're going to see how the pages can be formatted with HTML and CSS. You'll start with HTML.

1 Launch Dreamweaver if you closed it.

2 Choose File > Open, navigate to Lesson_02 folder and open **html_ formatting.html**.

3 Click the Split view button to see both the code and the design view.

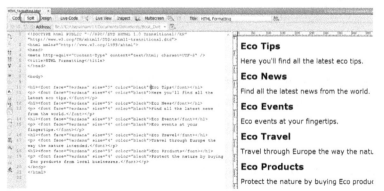

Inspect the code. Each element on the page uses a <font> tag, that is not used any more (it is deprecated). One of the attributes of this tag is color (notice the American English spelling).

```
</head>

<body>

<h1><font face="Verdana" size="5" color="black">Eco Tips</font></h1>
<p> <font face="Verdana" size="4" color="black">Here you'll find all the
latest eco tips.</font></p>
<h1><font face="Verdana" size="5" color="black">Eco News</font></h1>
<p> <font face="Verdana" size="4" color="black">Find all the latest news
from the world.</font></p>
<h1><font face="Verdana" size="5" color="black">Eco Events</font></h1>
```

4 Now, you'll change the colour of the text. To change the colour of the text, highlight the word black, and replace it with another colour, i.e. **green**.

5 Change all the headings to green by highlighting every color attribute for <h1> headings, and replacing the words black with **green**.

6 Click in the Design view to update the page. Notice that you don't have to change the view to Design, just click in the Design view, and Dreamweaver will update the preview of the page while you're working in the Split view.

7 Highlight one of the color attributes for one of the headings, and type in **gren** instead of green.

Notice, that now the colour of the heading doesn't change to green. That's how easy it is to make a mistake trying to format the page with HTML. It is also very slow, you need to change every single instance of the same attribute within your HTML code. Imagine having an HTML page with hundreds of lines of code and trying to change the colours of headings. Tedious work. In the next step, you'll start working with a CSS formatted page.

50

Formatting pages with CSS

So far you have managed to change styling of a page by using HTML formatting. Now it's time for some CSS, but first a few words about CSS. CSS is also a language, like HTML, and CSS was created to work in combination with HTML to apply styling to the content on a page.

For now, it is important that you understand that HTML and CSS are seperate languages that work very well together.

CSS (Cascading Style Sheets) was developed by the World Wide Web Consortium (W3C), and the latest official implementation of CSS specification is CSS2 (CSS3 is still work in progress, even though some web browsers support it already).

Let's move on to the next exercise.

Open **css_formatting.html** from the Lesson_02 folder.

When you look at the page in Design view, it looks almost identical to the previous file.

You will notice a big difference if you look at the page in the Code view.

9 Click the Split view button.

Now, notice the difference in structure of the document. The content looks identical, but this page is formatted with CSS. The CSS *rules*, as they're called, can be found in the head section of the page.

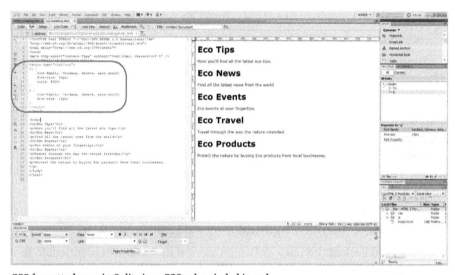

CSS formatted page in Split view, CSS rules circled in red.

The structure of the page remains the same: a heading followed by a paragraph, five headings and paragraphs in total. Look carefully in the CSS code and notice that there is only one rule for a heading <h1>, and it is applied to all the headings on the page.

Notice that all the headings are formatted as Verdana 36px in black (#000 is a hexadecimal value for black).

Say, you want the headings to be green as in previous exercise.

10 Navigate to the CSS Styles panel on the right side of the screen, and click on <h1> rule to highlight it.

CSS Syles panel has two buttons on the top. For now, just make sure that **All** is selected. CSS Styles panel is divided into two sections. When you highlight the rule in the top section called **All Rules**, the bottom section called **Properties** will display all the properties associated with this property.
(If you don't see the rules in the top section, and you see the plus sign (+) next to the word <style>, then click on it to expand it.)

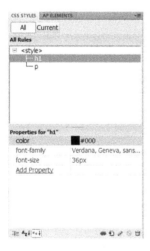
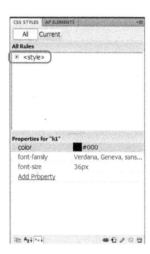

53

11 To change the colour of the headings, click on the colour swatch next to the property called color, and select a new colour from the swatches here:

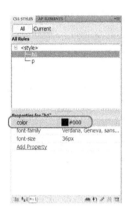 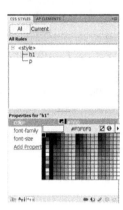

12 The colour updates instantly on the page, when you select a new colour from the swatches.

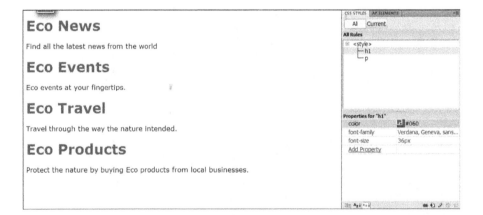

13 In this step, you're going to change the colour of the paragraph text.

Navigate back to the CSS Styles panel, and highlight the <p> rule in the

All Rules section.

This rule doesn't have a colour property, so it inherits the default colour (black). We'll talk more about CSS in later lessons, so for now just leave it the way it is.

Now you see how easy it is to format your page with CSS in Dreamweaver. CSS Styles panel is very easy to use and at the same time it is a powerful feature offering you the full control of your page formatting.

In the last step, you're going to change the default font family for all the text on the page. This page uses Verdana font, as you can see in the CSS Styles panel. Notice, that both CSS rules (<h1>, and <p>) have the font family defined.

55

14 Navigate to your CSS Styles panel, and highlight the **<h1>** rule in the top section (All Rules). In the bottom section (properties) highlight **font-family** property, and click on the drop-down menu next to it. The list of fonts will be revealed.

15 Go through the list and choose the font you like.

We will talk more about fonts in the future lesson, for now just choose one of the fonts from the list. Notice how the font instantly changes on the page. Because you changed the font family for the heading, only the headings update. In the next and your final step, you're going to change the font family for the paragraph text as well.

16 Navigate to your CSS Styles panel once again, and highlight the

<p> rule this time. In the bottom section, once again highlight the **font-family** property, and change it using the drop-down menu, that appears.

Notice how easy it is to assign a font family to your text on the page and how you can easily assign different fonts to your headings and paragraphs of text.

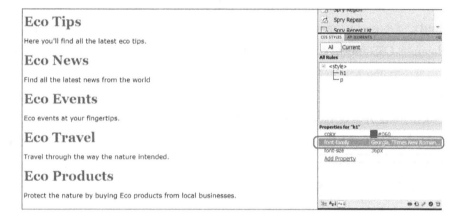

Congratulations! You have successfully finished another lesson.
Just before you finish with this chapter, I want to share a few more words about HTML and CSS with you.
Just turn the page over to the next page and find out a bit more about HTML/CSS relationship.

HTML was never intended to do all the customization/presentation of the web pages you were to create. HTML lacked a standard way to format the text and load the fonts (when we talk more about the fonts, you'll find out more on how to load the fonts dynamically from the internet to expand number of fonts you can use in your web pages).

Creating page layouts, as an example, was a very difficult task with HTML and required using the tables. Nowadays, we just use CSS for that and it is so much easier and more future proof than using HTML table-based layouts. HTML-based formatting was actually deprecated from the HTML language and CSS-based formatting was widely accepted as a proper way to design layouts. CSS allows you to limit your HTML code to just the content, and do all the styling within CSS.

Each of the HTML elements, there are around 100, comes with some default styling, that a web browser understands, so if you add an <h1> heading on a page, as an example, the web browser will style it as a big, bold text. You can overwrite it using CSS, and we will talk about that more in the future lessons.

Review Questions

1. What program can you use to open and edit HTML files?

2. What are the three main elements of every web page?

3. Where in Dreamweaver can you change the properties of text that uses CSS for styling?

Review Answers

1. HTML files can be opened and edited with HTML editors such as Adobe Dreamweaver as well as text editors (Notepad, TextEdit, and many more).

2. The three main elements of every web page are: Html, Head, and Body.

3. All CSS rules in Dreamweaver can be found in the CSS Styles panel.

Lesson 3

Quick Start - Set Up a Website

In this lesson you're going to familiarize with Dreamweaver's web building features and learn how to:

- Define new site settings

- Establish local root folder

- Create a new page using a CSS layout

- Modify the page title

- Insert Text from an external file

- Customise your page with CSS

This lesson will take about 1 hour 15 minutes to complete.

Setting Up a new Dreamweaver Site

The power of Dreamweaver lies in its ability to quickly and easily create websites and in its web management tools. You will be using Dreamweaver to create the complete website. The web pages created inside Dreamweaver will share the same layout and common elements. Once you've finished building your website, you can quickly upload it to the web server using Dreamweaver's fantastic upload features within Files panel.

A site, in Dreamweaver, refers to the local location (on your computer) where all the files that are used on a website are stored. Before you start creating web pages, you should define your site first.

Let's start by setting up a new site.

1 Launch Adobe Dreamweaver CS5, if it is not already open.

2 If you see the Welcome Screen, click on Dreamweaver Site button.

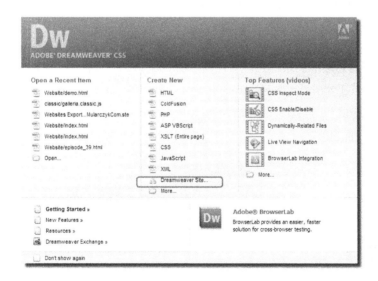

3   If you don't see the Welcome Screen (you may have disabled it through the Dreamweaver Properties), choose Site > New Site from the menu. The Site Setup dialogue box appears.

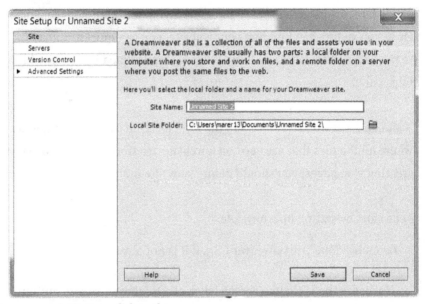

Dreamweaver's Site Setup dialogue box

If you have used Dreamweaver before, you will notice that the Site Setup dialogue box has changed in Dreamweaver CS5. It has been redesigned and simplified. Now, in Dreamweaver CS5, there are no Basic and Advanced views, and to create a new website you just need at least the name and the local site folder.

4   In the Site Name field, type **Lesson_03**.

Next, you will need to set up a Local Site Folder. This is a folder, where Dreamweaver stores the files you are working with (every page you create in Dreamweaver will be automatically saved within your Local Site Folder).

NOTE: Keep all the files you use on your website in the same main folder within your Local Site Folder to make sure, that when you upload the site to the web server the links will work properly.

5 In the Local Site Folder field, click on the folder icon to the right and navigate to the Lesson_03 folder containing the files for this lesson.

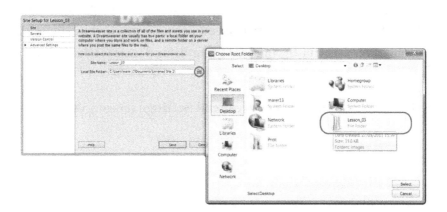

6 Select Lesson_03 folder, and click Open (Windows) or Choose (Mac). Then, click Select (Windows) or Choose (Mac) to choose this folder as your local root folder.

Before you click Save, we'll add one more piece of information. We'll point Dreamweaver to the images folder.

NOTE: Even though this is not required, it is a good practise to keep seperate content in seperate folders. It is very common to keep images, PDFs, videos, and sounds in seperate folders. That's why Dreamweaver helps you here by giving you option to define the images folder. If you define the images folder for your site, and later try to insert images from other locations, Dreamweaver will copy the images to your defined images folder within the site.

7 Click the arrow next to the **Advanced Settings** category on the left to reveal a list of tabs. Select **Local Info** category.

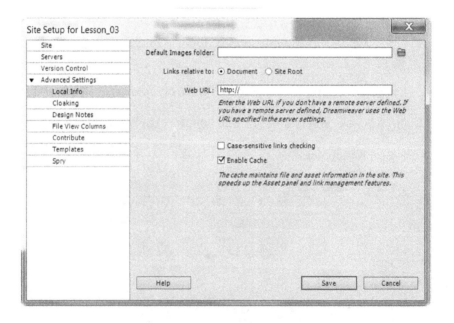

8 Next to **Default Images folder** field, click the folder icon. When the dialogue box opens, navigate to the images folder located inside Lesson_03 folder and click Select (Windows) or Choose (Mac).

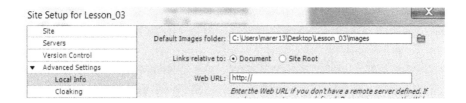

You have added all the required information and you're ready to start creating the first page.

In the Site Setup dialogue box click Save. Your Files panel should display the images folder and site name as on the screenshot on the left below.

NOTE: If you don't see the images folder, you may need to click on the icon next to the site name as it may be collapsed (as on the screenshot on the right).

Congratulations! You have defined your first site in Dreamweaver. Now, you're ready to create your first web page.

Create your first Web Page

Dreamweaver's Welcome screen gives you a quick access to a number of pages you can create. However, when you use Welcome screen to create a new HTML page, Dreamweaver will create a blank page. Give it a try to see what I mean.

10 On the Welcome screen, in the Create New column, click HTML to create a new HTML page.

11 Dreamweaver creates a new, blank HTML document as on the screenshot below:

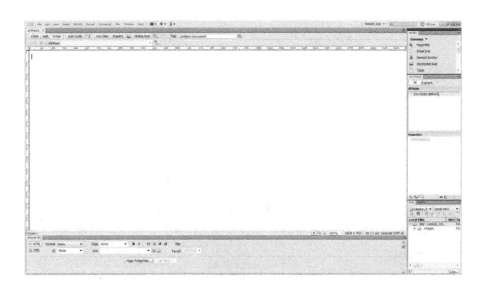

12 Close the document by choosing File > Close.

You're going to create a new HTML page using one of many presets that come with Dreamweaver to get a quick start in designing your first page. In the later lesson, we'll talk about creating web pages entirely from scratch using no presets at all.

68

Dreamweaver's CSS Starter pages

Dreamweaver CS5 comes with 16 layouts (starter pages) that use pure CSS/HTML - the best practise in web design. These starter pages were created by experts and were tested to make sure they work cross-platform in all major web browsers. All these starter pages are web standards compliant. Adobe included popular one, two, and three - column layouts in either fixed or liquid set ups. I hear you asking: "What's the difference between fixed and liquid layouts?" Here you go:

- Fixed layouts are specified in fixed dimensions in pixels, i.e. 950px wide;
- Liquid layouts are specified in relative measurements in percentage, i.e. 90% wide

Fixed layouts are more common as you can decide how wide your page is going to be and keep it that size all the time, i.e. 950px all the time. If you go for a liquid layout, your web page is going to change its width based on the viewer's browser window, i.e. when they resize their browser window or use a small screen, your page will resize (to keep it 90% width all the time). This may result in unwanted shift of the content of your page. A good example is Amazon website (*amazon.com* or *amazon.co.uk*). They used to use a liquid layout on their website even a few years ago, I still remember it. A few years ago, they made a move to a fixed layout as their content was moving within a liquid layout - they have a lot of content on their homepage and there are some buttons in the top right corner. Within a liquid layout these buttons were moving below the main menu, when you were resizing the browser window or using a small screen. It didn't look good.

You're going to use one of the starter pages and customise it.

69

13 Choose File > New.

14 In the New Document dialogue box that appears choose **Blank Page** in the first column.

15 In the following columns choose: **HTML**, and "**1 column fixed, centred, header and footer**".

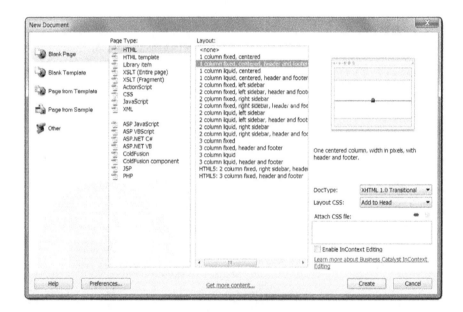

16 On the far right, you'll see the preview of the page with the description below it.

The preview displays a padlock icon, meaning that the width is set to fixed value in pixels. Leave all the other options on the defaults and click **Create**. Your new page will appear in Dreamweaver as a new document with some filler text. That's where you'll start customising the document.

70

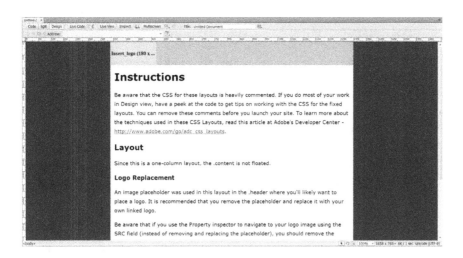

17 Highlight the big heading saying *Instructions*, delete it and type in

Welcome to EcoLiving.

This is the main heading for your brand new website! The reason why this heading is so big is because this line of text has been formatted as a Heading 1, which is the biggest heading in HTML (more on headings in later lesson). Now, you'll see how you can find out which type of heading this is and how to change it.

18 Put your cursor anywhere inside the big heading, and look into the Properties panel. The drop-down menu next to Formatting should say: **Heading 1**. If you want to make the heading smaller, you can change it to Heading 2 using the drop-down menu.

NOTE: You don't have to highlight the entire heading on the page, just put your cursor anywhere within the heading. That's because the headings are "block elements", which means they appear on a seperate line. Because of that, you don't have to highlight the entire line to make any adjustments to the formatting of the heading. It might be a good idea to save the page now.

19 Choose File > Save As... and type **myCSSpage.html** in the File Name field. Click Save.

There is a reason, why I asked you to save the page as myCSSpage.html. Let me follow with the explanation on the next page. There are a few rules you need to follow when saving your documents.

Naming Conventions in Web Design

There are some naming conventions or naming rules when you create your HTML documents that you need to follow. These naming conventions are common in web design, whether you use Dreamweaver or a text editor to create pages. To make sure you achieve consistency between different web browser and that your pages render correctly in all the web browsers, you need to follow these four rules when naming your HTML documents:

- no spaces - myCSSpage.html is correct, my CSS page.html is not,
- no special characters - no characters like: &, %, ?, !,
- do not start the name with a number - you can create a page called products2.html, but not 2products.html,
- do not start the name with a capital letter - myCSSpage.html is fine, MyCSSpage.html is not.

These are the four main rules for you to follow. Now that you've saved the page, you're going to preview it in a web browser.

20 Choose File > Preview in Browser to preview your page in a web browser. Choose the browser from the list that appears next to Preview in Browser.

21 Now you'll replace the text on the page. Navigate back to Dreamweaver, and highlight all the text below the heading (keep the text that says footer at the bottom of the page - see the screenshot on the next page).

22 Press Delete key on your keyboard to remove the highlighted text.

Now, you'll add new text to the page. Inside the images folder, you'll find a text file called **homepage.rtf**. You're going to open this file, copy and paste the text from this file onto the page in Dreamweaver.

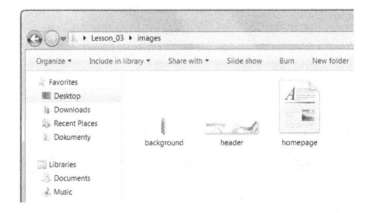

23 Navigate to the folder on your computer as shown on the screenshot on the previous page, and double click on the text file to open it with your default text editor.

It is not important what text editor you're using to open the file. You can copy and paste the text between any text editor and Dreamweaver. Dreamweaver doesn't open RTF files.

24 Copy all the text in your text editor by highlighting it and choosing Ctrl+C on Windows / Cmd+C on Mac, or by using Edit > Copy.

25 Navigate back to Dreamweaver, and choose Edit > Paste Special. You will see the dialogue box as on the screenshot below.

The reason I asked you to choose Edit > Paste Special, and not Edit > Paste or Ctrl+V on Windows / Cmd+V on Mac, is so you could make a choice how you want to import the text from the clipboard.

As you can see on the screenshot, you can paste the text as **Text Only** (no formatting) or **Text with structure** (formatted text). We'll talk more about the options here a bit later on.

26 Choose **Text with structure**, and click OK.

27 To add more space at the bottom of the page (before the footer) put your cursor in the last line of the text, and press Enter on your keyboard.

Insert_logo (180 x ...

Welcome to EcoLiving

Try to approach a number of people and ask them why they don't adopt an eco/green lifestyle and see what they say. They usually say things like "It's too expensive." or "It requires too much effort and self-discipline." This could not be further from truth.
Today, it is so much easier and cheaper to go eco and green. It is so easy to buy organic fruit and vegetables, recycled paper etc. Many stores nowadays sell a big variety of ogranic food and recycled paper products.
If you want to turn green, you came to the right place! Here you will find all the useful information you need and we'll show you how easy it is to go green!
We hope you'll enjoy our website and if you do, let your friends know about it.

Footer

The technique you have just used, is not a good way to add space on your pages and I am going to show you a proper way of doing it (and with more control as well). However, this will require some CSS knowledge so for now you'll just use Enter key on the keyboard.

28 It's time for a page title. Navigate to the Title field on the top of the document window, and highlight the text that currently reads *Untitled Document*.

29 Replace it with **Go Eco-friendly with EcoLiving** and press Enter/Return.

30 Save the page by choosing File > Save or using keyboard shortcut Ctrl+S on Windows / Cmd+S on Mac.

Now, you'll add another heading on a page and a paragraph of text below it. This time, you will type it instead of copying and pasting.

31 Insert your cursor at the end of the last line of text that ends with ".. let your friends know about it.", and press Enter/Return.

32 Type **Contribute to our Community**.

33 With the cursor still on the same line, navigate to the Properties panel and change formatting to **Heading 3**.

34 Press Enter/Return, and type the following text below the heading:

```
If you enjoy our website and the message we're trying
to pass to others, join our Community and share your
knowledge with us by becoming a contributor to the web-
site.
```

The text automatically becomes a paragraph text, as indicated by the Properties Panel. Now, you'll customise the footer.

35 Highlight the text *footer* at the bottom of the page in the fetor section. Delete it and insert the copyright symbol by choosing Insert > HTML > Special Characters > Copyright.

36 Next to the copyright symbol, that appears now in the footer, type

2011 EcoLiving.org. All rights reserved.

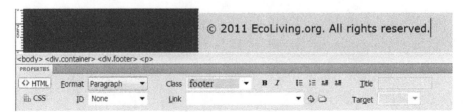

In the next step, you're going to remove the image placeholder and add an image in the header of the page instead.

37 Navigate to the top of the page, and click on the *Insert_logo* image

placeholder in the header to highlight it.

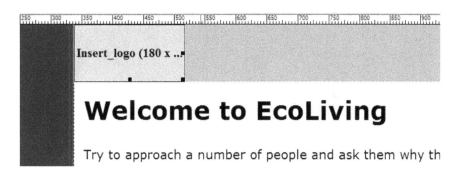

38 Press Delete key on your keyboard to delete it.

39 Choose Insert > Image, and navigate to the images folder. Choose

the **header** image, and click OK.

40 Now, you'll get prompted for Accessibility Attributes. Type

EcoLiving header image, and press OK.

Congratulations! You have successfully inserted an image into the header on the page. Your page starts looking better. There is only one challenge here. The image is a bit narrower than the page itself. As resizing graphics within Dreamweaver is not advised, you have two options:

○ you could resize the graphic in Photoshop or Fireworks
○ you could resize the page in Dreamweaver

You're going to use the second option here as we will be talking about Photoshop and Fireworks in future lessons. Besides, it is a good opportunity to do some CSS work. You'll see how easy it is. First, you need to find out which rule defines the width of page and what is the width of header image.

41 Highlight the header image on the page and check the size using the Properties panel as shown on the screenshot on the next page.

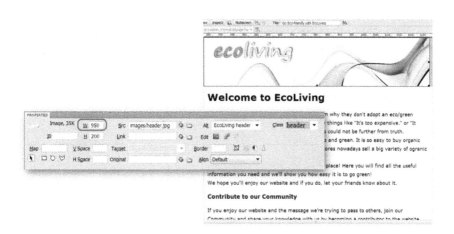

The image is 950px wide. Now, you'll check which rule defines the width of the page and change it to 950px as well.

42 With image still highlighted look at the bottom left corner of your document window. See the tag inspector displaying a number of HTML tags. That's how you'll find out which rule defines the width of the page.

Here's what it says:
- the highlighted element on the page is an image **<img>**, positioned within parent element - a Div tag with a class header **<div.header>**,
- this element is positioned inside another element, another Div tag with a class container **<div.container>**

This means that it is the container rule, that will define the page width.

81

43 Navigate to the CSS Styles panel and highlight the **.container** rule in the **All Rules** section. Click next to width property in the Properties section, and type **950** instead of 960. Done.

Now that you've created a page in Dreamweaver, it's time to specify some default formatting options for the page through CSS.

44 Navigate to CSS Styles panel and click **body** rule in **All Rules** section. In the bottom section (Properties) click on the little pencil icon to edit the properties of the body rule (body rule defines defaults for the page).

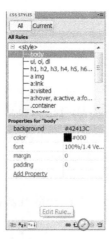

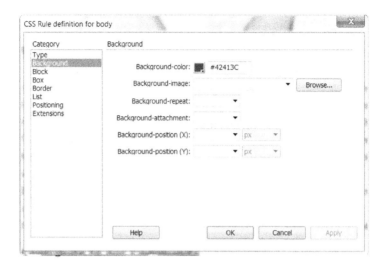

In the dialogue box that opens you'll set up some default for the web page. The CSS Rule definition dialog box displays eight different categories that format different aspects of your page. You'll start by setting the default options for the text on the page using the Type category.

45 Select Type category on the left to display text options for the page.

In this dialogue box, you'll set all the defaults for the text on the page. Look at the dialogue box and notice the options that appear here. You'll be using this dialogue box to define page defaults (later on entire website defaults as well), and to modify the settings that have been already created.

46 Start by defining the default font family that you want to use for your page. Choose one of the font lists from the drop-down menu, and click Apply to change it without closing the dialogue box. Notice how the font changes.

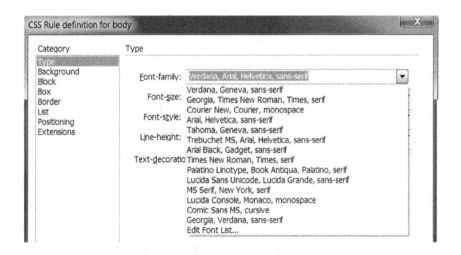

NOTE: We'll talk more about the fonts in the future lesson. You may have noticed that when you select the drop-down menu next to **Font-family**, a limited number of fonts appears on this list. You will find out why in the lesson on text. For now, just choose one of the fonts you like from the drop-down menu.

47 Change the spacing between the lines of text by changing the Line-height property, as highlighted on the screenshot on the next page.

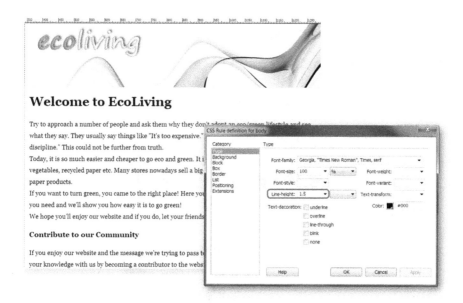

48 Once you're done, click OK.

Changing the website's background colour.

There's one more task for you before we finish this lesson. You're going to change the website's background colour, the colour that appears behind the page (dark grey). This colour will also be defined in CSS, so you're going to use the CSS Styles panel to change it.

49 Navigate to the CSS Styles panel and find the rule called **body** (the same rule you have just customised to change the font). Body rule defines the colour that appears behind your page. Once you've highlighted the **body** rule in the **All Rules** section, click on the little pencil icon at the bottom of the panel to edit the rule.

85

50 Select the **Background** category on the left, and notice the

Background-color property. That's where you change it.

51 Click on the colour swatch next to Background-color property, and

when the color palette appears, choose the light pastel colour swatch.

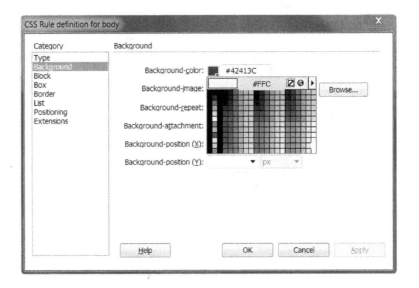

52 After selecting a colour, click OK to accept the changes. You have

changed the colour that appears behind your page. You're done.

53 Save the page and preview your final result in the web browser. Then,

close the page.

Congratulations! You have successfully finished this lesson.

Review Questions

1. What characters you shouldn't use when naming your pages?

2. What are the best practices to save the pages with more than one word i.e. *Contact Us* page?

3. What's the reason for setting up the local Site folder?

4. What are Dreamweaver's CSS Starter pages?

Review Answers

1. When naming your pages, you shouldn't use any special characters, i.e. ?, !, &, %.

2. When saving the pages with more than one word in the name, you can use an underscore, i.e. *contact_us.html*, or put both words together, i.e. *contactus.html*.

3. You should keep all the files you use on your website in the same main folder within your Local Site Folder to make sure, that when you upload the site to the web server the links will work properly.

4. Dreamweaver's CSS Starter pages use pure CSS/HTML - the best practise in web design. These starter pages were created by experts and were tested to make sure they work cross-platform in all major web browsers. All these starter pages are web standards compliant.

Lesson 4

Create a Page Layout

In this lesson you're going to familiarize with Dreamweaver's page layout techniques and learn how to:

- Plan your page layout

- Customise a pre-defined CSS layout

- Preview pages using Live view

- Add text based menu

- Modify the footer with CSS

- Wrap text around an image

This lesson will take about 1 hour 15 minutes to complete.

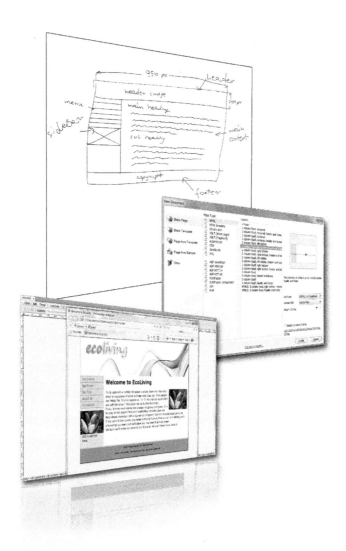

Plan your Page Layout

Before you start designing your website in Dreamweaver, you need to decide on the purpose of your website. This one question will define how the pages are going to be layed out. And the second most important question you need to ask yourself is the audience of your website. Your layout will depend on these two things. The amount of content will also define the layout of the pages. Is your website going to display information for your visitors or maybe it is going to sell some products? What age are your primary visitors? Are they adults, teenagers, children?

If you're designing with teenagers/children in mind, your website will need to be very engaging and interactive. The website with older people in mind will look totally different.

It's usually a good idea to start by doing some research. In our case, we're designing a website for a fictitious eco/organic charity organisation that wants to increase audience's awareness on the topic of ecology, recycling, and green lifestyle.

Your audience

Find out more about your audience before you start building your website. Ask yourself these few questions:

- what internet connection are visitors using (high-speed, dial-up)?
- what web browser are they likely to use?
- what is the screen resolution of their display?

If someone is using a slow internet connection, they don't want to wait for all your fancy animations and graphics to load. What if they use a mobile phone? They may not have Flash Player, so you may want to use graphics or JQuery for some nice animations instead of Flash animations.

What about different operating systems and web browsers? You can find some interesting statistics on the W3C website (World Wide Web Consortium). Here are some statistics from W3C:

- Operating systems' market share:
  Windows - ca.80%
  Mac OS - ca.10%
  Linux - ca.10%
- Web browsers market share (Jan 2011):
  Mozilla Firefox - 44%
  Internet Explorer - 28%
  Google Chrome - 20%
  Apple Safari - 4%
- Current average screen resolution is 1024 x 768 px (computers)

With mobile devices, it is more tricky as there are many mobile phones with so many different screen resolutions and different web browsers (most mobile phones have their own web browsers). More and more people use their mobile phones to access the internet and they use their mobile phones more frequently than their computers (for internet access). This brings a challenge to web designers, because they need to keep in mind mobile users nowadays as well.

The website we're working on here, is a website for a fictitious charity dedicated to sharing their knowledge of eco living with their visitors. This means, that the visitors will come from different backgrounds and different age groups. After doing some research, you also found out that your vistors are primarily using desktop and laptop computers, with about 20% of visitors using their mobile devices (mobile phones and tablets).

Wireframing

Once you've decided on your audience, you need to decide on the number of pages within your website, and how they're going to look like. That's wireframing.

Start by creating thumbnails (you can do it on a piece of paper) for the pages. Thumbnails should include the connections between the pages as shown below:

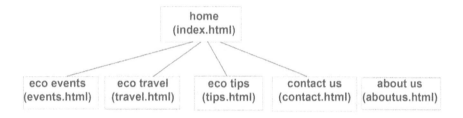

Notice that the visitor can navigate to every page from a home page. There will be links between all the pages as well.

The next step will be to create a visual representation of the website's layout. Try to figure out what your website will look like. How many columns will you need? Will you position the sidebar on the left or on the right? What will you present in the sidebar? What about the positioning of the objects? It is very important where you put the content on your website. On the next page, you'll find out where the "EcoLiving" team decided to put the content on the website.

Because in the western culture people read from left to right, and from top to bottom, EcoLiving website will have two-column layout with a sidebar on the left. The sidebar will hold the menu, and the right column will be the main content area on the page. The website will also be centre-aligned within a web browser window.

Some companies like their websites to be left-aligned to the edge of the browser window, however, if someone uses a high-resolution screen (1900px wide or more), they will see a lot of empty space on the right. If you centre your website (EcoLiving website is going to be 950px wide), a person using 1900px wide screen will see 500px space on the left and 500px space on the right.

Here's a wireframe for EcoLiving website:

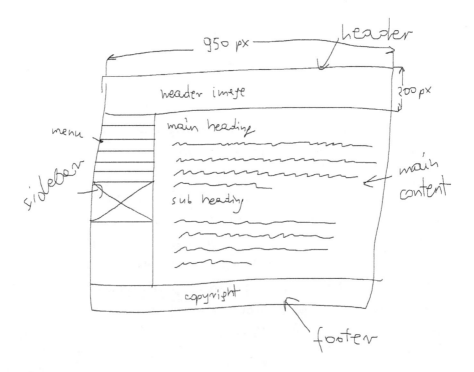

You may also want to create a mockup of a website in Adobe Photoshop or Fireworks, so here's one as well:

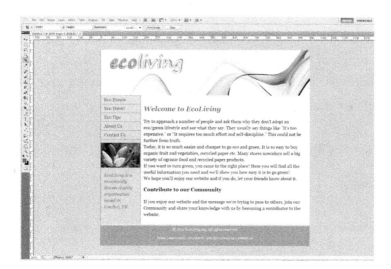

This is just a mockup, so it may change during the discussions with your client. This is the initial mockup with ideas for a website. The mockup that was created with Adobe Photoshop or Fireworks can be easily exported as a JPEG or a PNG file, and easily viewed on any computer or mobile device.

NOTE: For a ling time, designers were using Fireworks to create mockups and they were exporting their mockups to CSS based layouts with fully functional menus, links, and hotspots. This is one of the advantages of Fireworks over Photoshop. However, nowadays we primarily use Fireworks or Photoshop to create mockups to present them to the client and then we build the website in Dreamweaver.

Now it's time you started building a layout using of the starter pages that come with Dreamweaver and customising it.

95

Customise a pre-defined CSS layout

The predefined CSS Starter pages are a good point to start in the process of creating pages. They're fantastic at this stage of your learning process as you don't know how to create page layout from scratch yet. Don't worry, you will learn how to do it in the future lesson. For now, CSS Starter pages are quick to create and easy to customise.

You'll start by finding a layout that matches your design using the starter pages.

1   Launch Adobe Dreamweaver CS5, if it is not already open.

2   If you see the Welcome Screen, click on Dreamweaver Site button to

define a new Site. If you don't see the Welcome Screen (you may have

disabled it through the Dreamweaver Properties), choose Site > New Site

from the menu. The Site Setup dialogue box appears.

3   In the Site Name field, type **Lesson_04**.

4   In the Local Site Folder field, click on the folder icon to the right and

navigate to the **Lesson_04** folder containing the files for this lesson.

5   Select **Lesson_04** folder, and click Open (Windows) or Choose (Mac).

Then, click Select (Windows) or Choose (Mac) to choose this folder as your

local root folder.

Click the arrow next to the **Advanced Settings** category on the left to reveal a list of tabs. Select **Local Info** category and next to **Default Images folder** field, click the folder icon. When the dialogue box opens, navigate to the images folder located inside Lesson_04 folder and click Select (Windows) or Choose (Mac).

In the Site Setup dialogue box click Save. Your Files panel should display the images folder and site name as on the screenshot below.

Choose File > New, and when the New Document dialogue box opens choose: Blank Page, HTML, and "**2 fixed, left sidebar, header and footer**" as a layout.

If you inspect the layouts that come with Dreamweaver, you'll notice that the one you've selected in this step looks almost identical to the mockup from the beginning of the chapter. That's the one you're going to customise now.

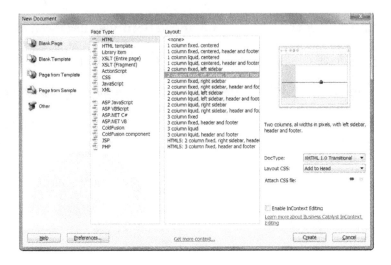

9 With the Layout highlighted, notice the preview in the top right corner

and the description below.

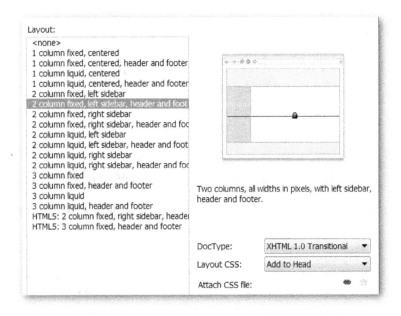

10 Keep all the other settings on their defaults and click **Create**. The

explanation of the other settings on the next page.

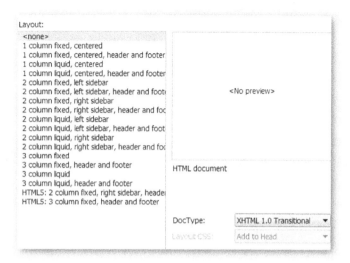

DocType declaration

When the document you create is an HTML or XHTML document, it is important to add a DocType declaration. Unfortunately, there is not just one type of HTML, so there are a number of different declarations: HTML 4.01 Strict, HTML 4.01 Trasitional, XHTML 1.0 Strict, and more. All these declarations are defined in the W3C specifications, you just need to add a proper declaration to your page so the web browser will know how to render the page properly.

Why is it so important?

You may ask why you should bother with that. Well, you don't really have to because Dreamweaver will take care of it for you, you just need to know which DocType you'll be using and set it as a default in Dreamweaver. DocType defines which version of (X)HTML your document is using. This is a very important piece of information as specifying the DocType will allow some tools like Markup Validator to check the syntax of your document. Specifying a DocType will also make your life easier as the web browser will know which DocType you're using and will render your content properly.

Why XHTML 1.0?

XHTML is a family of document types based on HTML 4, and they extend what HTML 4 can do. The documents in XHTML are written to operate better than HTML 4 documents. XHTML documents are the next step in the evolution of the Internet. One of the new features within XHTML is that the documents need to be well formed (you need to be careful with that if using a text editor , if you use Dreamweaver, Dreamweaver will take care of it for you). A quick example would be the naming conventions:

◦ XHTML documents must use lower case for all HTML elements and attributes.

XHTML 1.0 is a default DocType in Dreamweaver as it became a W3C recommendation in 2000.

How to change the default DocType in Dreamweaver?

Here's where you can change the default DocType in Dreamweaver:

◦ Edit > Preferences on Windows, Dreamweaver > Preferences on Mac,
◦ New Document category.

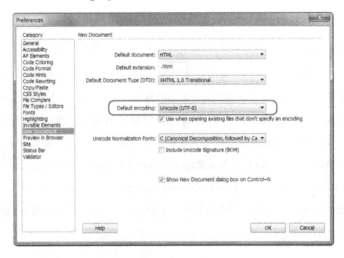

11 Back to the project, once you clicked Create, a new page appears in the Design view in Dreamweaver.

This page uses CSS to manage the layout. Let's what it looks like when you turn off the CSS. Yes, I'm not kidding, you can actually "turn off" CSS to see what the page looks like without any styling applied to it.

12 Choose View > Style Rendering > Display Styles to turn styling off.

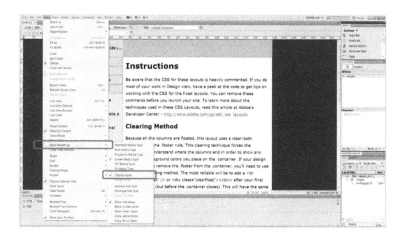

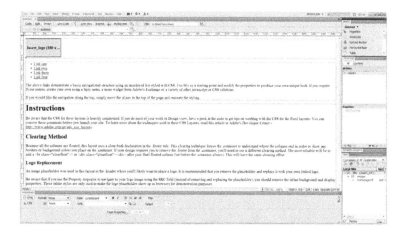

13 All the styling disappeared! That's what the page looks like as an HTML page with no styling attached to it. What you're looking at is just an HTML page with content and no layout. Turn CSS back by choosing View > Style Rendering > Display Styles.

14 Delete the image placeholder (Insert_logo) in the header section of the page by selecting the image and pressing Delete key on the keyboard.

This time, instead of inserting image on the page, you're going to add a header image as a background image through CSS. This technique will also require defining the height of the header. You may have noticed that the height of the header changed when you deleted the image placeholder.

15 Navigate to the CSS Styles panel, and select header rule in the All Rules section on the top of the panel.

NOTE: If you don't see the rules in the All Rules section, just the word <style>, click on the plus sign (+) next to it to expand the rules with a stylesheet.

16 With the header rule selected, click on the little pencil icon at the bottom of the CSS Styles panel to edit this rule.

17 Select Background category and click Browse next to Background-image property. Select **header** image and press OK. If you see a message saying that you should save your document first, just click OK. You'll save it in just a moment.

18 Click Apply to see how the header image appears on the page.

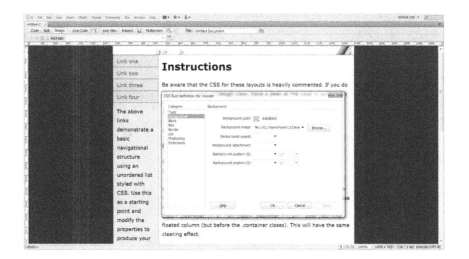

19 To change the height of the header, select **Box** category, and type 200px for Height. Click OK.

20 Save the page as **index.html**.

21 Highlight the main heading on the page and replace it with **Welcome to EcoLiving**.

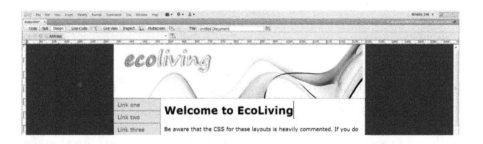

22 Highlight all the text on the page, below the main heading and delete it.

23 Navigate to the Files panel (it should be located below the CSS Styles panel), and double click on **homepage.rtf** file to open it. It will open with your default text editor for RTF files.

24 Highlight all the text within the file and copy it. Back in Dreamweaver place your cursor below the main heading and paste the text into Dreamweaver (Edit > Paste or Ctrl/Cmd+V).

25 Now, you'll customise the width of the page as it is a bit wider than the header graphic. Place your cursor in the right column on the page and look into the tag inspector to find out which rule defines the page's width (the container for all page elements).

It's the Div tag with a class **.container**. To change the width of the page, you need to change the width of the **container**.

26 Select the **.container** rule in the CSS Styles panel, and click on the

edit icon.

27 Select **Box** category, change width from 960px to **950px**. Press OK.

Now the width of the page looks right, but the column on the right dropped down below the sidebar column on the left. This happened because the total width of both columns is now bigger than the width of the page. Let's check it. Start by checking the width of the left column (sidebar).

28 In the CSS Styles panel select **.sidebar1** rule, and check its width.

Then do the same with the right column - **.content** rule. Both rules are

displayed on the screenshots below.

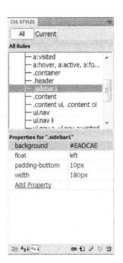 

Notice, that the width of the sidebar is 180px, and the width of the content is 780px, which makes it 960px in total. The page's width is 950px, that's why the right column moved below the sidebar as there is not enough space here.

Because there is not enough space for both columns, you need to resize one of them. One of the columns needs to have 10px subtracted from its width. Because the sidebar is narrow - it's only 180px, resize the right column - the content.

29 Select **.content** rule in the CSS Styles panel, and click on the value next to the width property as indicated on the screenshot below. Change the width to 770px.

Now the content moves back to where it belongs and the page is nicely laid out. Now, it's time to change the colour of the background behind the web page.

30 Select the **body** rule in the CSS Styles panel, and click on the pencil icon to edit the rule.

31 In the Rule Definition dialogue box that opens, select Background category, and change the background colour by clicking on the colour swatch next to the **Background-color** property. Click OK.

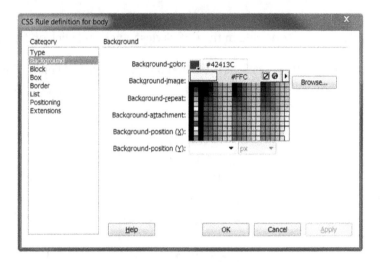

32 In this step, you're going to add a border around the web page so it looks like it has a shadow behind it. Select **.container** rule in the CSS Styles panel, and edit it.

33 In the Rule Definition dialogue box that appears select **Border** category.

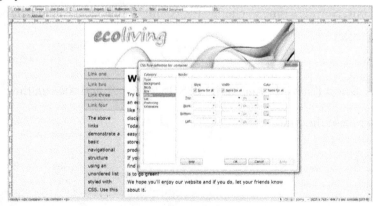

To create like a shadow effect, you're going to use different values for different sides of the container. Shadow usually only appears on two sides, so you're going to add a "shadow" effect on right and bottom.

34 In the Border category, leave the option "Same for all" checked for Style and Color, and set the Style to **ridge**, and Color to dark grey.

 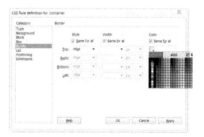

35 In the Width property, deselect "Same for all", and type: 1px for left and top, 3px for right and bottom. Click OK.

This time you're going to use a different method to preview the page in the web browser.

Preview pages in a Web browser

Dreamweaver does a really good job rendering the page in the Design view, however nothing will replace a real web browser. Dreamweaver can preview your pages in any web browser that's installed on your computer. If Dreamweaver doesn't detect one of your web browser, you can add it manually. That's what you're going to do now. In a moment, we'll also talk about Live view within Dreamweaver that allows you to preview the pages within Dreamweaver interface.

36 With the page still open, navigate to the top of the document window, and click on the little Globe icon. The drop-down menu will appear next to it displaying available web browsers. Choose one of the web browsers from the list and the page will open in the selected web browser.

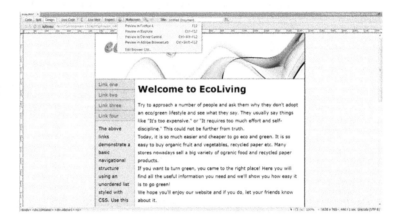

Notice the difference between the preview in Dreamweaver and preview in a web browser. There are some slight variations, but remember that it is the web browser that counts as that's what your visitors will use to navigate to your website.

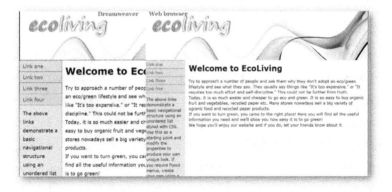

Live View

As you have noticed, Design view in Dreamweaver doesn't provide an accurate preview, and using a web browser every single time is time consuming. To save time, Dreamweaver CS4 introduced Live view that does a good job previewing pages so you don't have to open a web browser every single time. Sometimes you will be using a web browser, but in many cases Live view will be sufficient. And it's really quick to preview the pages in a Live view. You're going to try it now.

37 Back in Dreamweaver with the page still open, click the Live view button in the toolbar on the top of the document window.

Live view replaces standard Design view and displays browser like preview using WebKit browser engine found in Google Chrome and Apple Safari. If the page has rollover menu, you can preview it in the Live view. If the page has Flash animation, it will play.

Move cursor over menu on left and notice how the rollover effect appears.

It's time to customize the menu on the left.

38 Exit Live view by clicking on Live view button.

Customise the Menu

39 Back to Design view, highlight the first menu element "Link one", and replace it by typing **Eco Events**.

40 Replace the other menu elements by highlighting them and typing new name to get the menu as on the screenshot here:

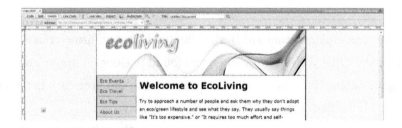

112

41 You need one more menu item. Here's an easy way to add it. Go to Split view by clicking on Split view button, and in the Design view part highlight the last menu item. The piece of code that's displaying this menu item will be highlighted in the Code view.

42 In the Code view highlight the entire line with the text highlighted (line 156) and copy it to the clipboard (Ctrl+C on Windows, Cmd+C on Mac).

43 Place your cursor at the end of line 156 (still in the Code view), and press Enter to move the cursor to the new line and add space.

44 Press Ctrl+V on Windows or Cmd+V on Mac to paste the code from the clipboard.

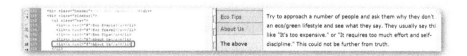

45 Highlight the text that reads: **About Us**, and replace it with **Contact Us.**

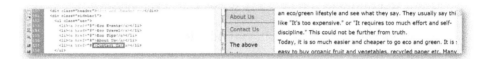

46 Click on Design view button to go back to Design view. The menu should update and display the last menu item you have just added.

Modify the footer with CSS

47 Scroll the page down so you can see the footer, highlight all the text in the footer and delete it.

48 With the cursor blinking in the footer, choose Insert > HTML > Special Characters > Copyright.

49 Next to the copyright symbol, type **2011 EcoLiving.org. All rights reserved.**

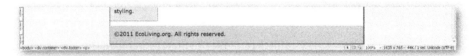

Directly below you'll add a text-based menu. It is a very common practise to add text-based menu at the bottom of the page to give visitors another way of browsing through the website as well as it increases the visibility (and ranking) of your website in search engines.

114

50 With your cursor at the end of the line in the footer press Enter/ Return to move to the next line and type the following menu items seperated by vertical line (pipe):

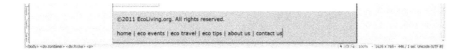

NOTE: The pipe symbol (|) is usually located next to the Shift key on your keyboard and you usually insert the symbol by holding the Shift key down and pressing the pipe key at the same time.

Customising the Footer with CSS

It's time to customise the footer using CSS. You're going to centre the text, customise the font, and add background colour and background image.

51 Find which rule manages the footer by leaving your cursor blinking in the footer and looking into the tag inspector at the bottom of the document window. It should look like this:

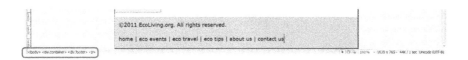

52 The rule managing the footer is a Div tag with a class **.footer**. Find the **.footer** rule in the CSS Styles panel and edit it by clicking on the pencil icon at the bottom of the CSS Styles panel.

115

53 To centre the text in the footer navigate to the **Block** category, and set

Text-align property to: **center**. Click Apply.

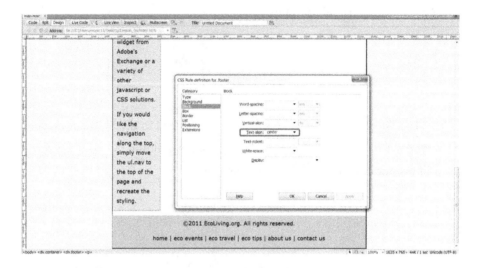

54 Footer text is now centred, but it's too big. Footer text should be small,

so it doesn't distract the viewer from the content on the page. Select **Type**

category on the left and set the **Font-size** property to **12px**. Click Apply.

55 Now you're going to add a background image in the footer. Still with the Rule Definition dialogue box open, select the **Background** category and click on the folder icon next to **Background-image** property.

56 Navigate to images folder and select the image **background.jpg**. Click OK and then Apply in the Rule Definition dialogue box.

57 Still in the **Background** category, from the **Background-repeat** drop-down menu choose: **repeat-x** and click Apply.

Now the image only repeats horizontally. It is a very common technique used by web designers when you use a tiny graphic prepared in Photoshop or Fireworks, that's usually less than 1kB in size, and then you tell the web browser through CSS to repeat the image either horizontally or vertically.

To make the footer look nice, you're going to set the footer background colour to the same colour as the bottom of the background image. Before proceeding to the next step, make sure you can see the footer so the Rule Definition dialogue box doesn't obstruct the view of the footer.

58 Still in the Background category, click on the colour swatch next to the **Background-color** property, and when the colour picker appears, move your cursor over the footer on the page (your cursor will change to the eyedropper icon as on the screenshot on the next page), and click on the bottom of the background graphic to sample the colour.

118

59 Click Apply.

The footer is done. Now it's time to style the sidebar. You'll start by removing the text from the sidebar as it is too long.

60 Highlight all the text below the menu in the sidebar and press Delete key to remove it.

61 With the cursor below the menu you'll insert image this time using the Insert panel. Navigate to the Insert panel and set the drop-down menu at the top to **Common**. Find **Images** button below and click on the arrow next to it so the drop-down menu appears. Select Image.

119

62 In Select Image Source dialogue box choose **flower.jpg** and click OK.

63 In the Image Tag Accessibility Attributes dialogue box that appears you'll add Alternate Text. Type **Flower image** and press OK.

NOTE: Image Tag Accessibility Attributes dialogue box appears when inserting images to add additional information for users with screen readers, so you should always add alternative text. Alternative text would also be used by the web browser if the image doesn't display on the page (it may be missing from the server or it may still be loading), so instead of seeing nothing, your visitors will see the alternative text.

64 If your layout shifted, you'll fix it now. It happens if the image is inserted inside the paragraph. You're going to position it before the paragraph of text. The screenshot on the next page shows an example of what happens when the image is inserted into a paragraph.

120

65 Select the image by clicking on it and click on the Split view button to see the code as well as the design. Notice an opening <p> tag before the image, this caused the shift on a page.

66 Highlight the **<p>** tag in the code view, cut it (Ctrl+X / Cmd+X), put your cursor after the highlighted code for image (just before closing **</p>** tag, and paste it (Ctrl+V / Cmd+V).

67 Click on the Design view button to go back to Design view and the page should now look good. If it still doesn't look good, preview the page in a web browser as it may be just a rendering in Dreamweaver as shown on the screenshot below (Dreamweaver on the left):

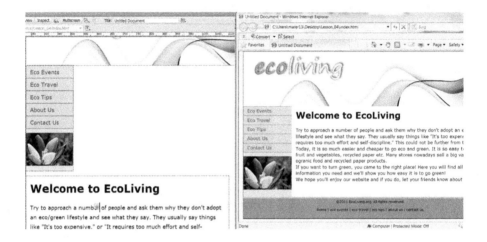

NOTE: After restarting Dreamweaver the preview usually goes back to normal.

68 Add some text in the sidebar below the image. Here's an easy way to put your cursor below the image. Click on the image to highlight it and press down arrow key on your keyboard to move the cursor below the image.

69 Type **Add a caption here.**

70 This is the last part of the lesson. You'll add an image on the page in the right column. Place your cursor at the beginning of the first paragraph below the main heading.

122

71 Insert an image by navigating to the Insert panel and clicking on

Images > **Image**. Choose **flower.jpg** once again.

72 When the Image Tag Accessibility Attributes dialogue box opens,

type **Flower image** and press OK.

73 To align the image to the right so the text could float around the

image, you'll use on the CSS classes that come with CSS starter pages. In

the later lessons you will be creating these classes. Now, with the image

selected navigate to the Properties panel and from the **Class** drop-down

menu choose **fltrt**. Now the image is floated to the right.

74 Finish the lesson with a web page title. In the Title section on the top of the document window type **Welcome to EcoLiving**.

75 Save and preview the page in a web browser. Here's your final result. Congratulations! You have successfully finished Lesson 4.

124

Review Questions

1. What is the current average screen resolution?

2. What applications can you use to create a mockup of a website?

3. Why is specifying a DocType of your document so important?

4. How does Live view differ from Design view?

Review Answers

1. Current average screen resolution is 1024 x 768 px (computers).

2. You can create a mockup of a website in Adobe Photoshop or Fireworks.

3. Specifying the DocType will allow some tools like Markup Validator to check the syntax of your document. Specifying a DocType will also make your life easier as the web browser will know which DocType you're using and will render your content properly.

4. Live view displays browser like preview using WebKit browser engine found in Google Chrome and Apple Safari.

Lesson 5

Working with Text and Tables

In this lesson you're going to start working with text and learn how to:

- Insert Headings and Paragraphs

- Add text from other sources

- Create Ordered and Unordered Lists

- Format text with CSS

- Add Tables

This lesson will take about 1 hour 30 minutes to complete.

Headings and Paragraphs

In HTML, there are six headings' tags - <h1>, <h2>, <h3>, <h4>, <h5>, and <h6>. Every web browser will format the content between one of these tags as a heading. Headings are used to organise the page into meaningful sections. If you look through any book, you'll notice that every chapter has a title or the chapter number as a heading. The same with web pages.

<h1> heading in HTML has the most semantic meaning and it is also the biggest on the page. All other headings are descending in order with <h6> being the less important among headings and being the smallest as well.

On your web page, the name of the page will appear as the main heading, and the subheadings will appear as <h2> elements.

1. Launch Adobe Dreamweaver CS5, if it is not already open.

2. If you see the Welcome Screen, click on Dreamweaver Site button to define a new Site. If you don't see the Welcome Screen (you may have disabled it through the Dreamweaver Properties), choose Site > New Site from the menu. The Site Setup dialogue box appears.

3. In the Site Name field, type **Lesson_05**.

4. In the Local Site Folder field, click on the folder icon to the right and navigate to the **Lesson_05** folder containing the files for this lesson.

5 Select **Lesson_05** folder, and click Open (Windows) or Choose (Mac). Then, click Select (Windows) or Choose (Mac) to choose this folder as your local root folder.

6 Click the arrow next to the **Advanced Settings** category on the left to reveal a list of tabs. Select **Local Info** category and next to **Default Images folder** field, click the folder icon. When the dialogue box opens, navigate to the images folder located inside Lesson_05 folder and click Select (Windows) or Choose (Mac).

7 In the Site Setup dialogue box click Save.

Here's the structure of the Lesson 05 in the Files panel:

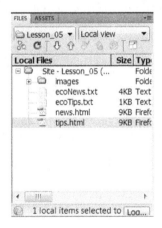

8 Choose File > Open, and select **news.html**.

9 When the page opens, select the waterfall image on the right and delete it by pressing Delete key on your keyboard.

Now, you're going to add text on the page using one of the text files provided. There are two .txt files within the website folder.

10 Double click on **ecoNews.txt** in the Files panel to open it. Notice that it opened within Dreamweaver! Dreamweaver can open .txt files.

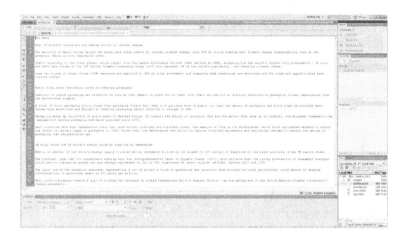

11 Click and drag to highlight the text. Next copy the highlighted text into the clipboard (Edit > Copy or Ctrl+C, Cmd+C).

12 Back to news.html, place the cursor in the right column on the page and paste the text (Edit > Paste or Ctrl+V, Cmd+V).

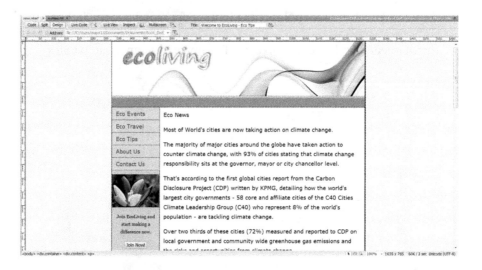

Now you'll start formatting the page. The first line that reads Eco News will become the main heading and the next line will be a subheading as a title for an article.

13 Click and drag to highlight the text Eco News. Now you'll format it using the Properties panel.

132

14 In the Properties panel, click on HTML button on the left to access the HTML formatting options. Choose Heading 1 from the Format drop-down menu. The text becomes bold and big.

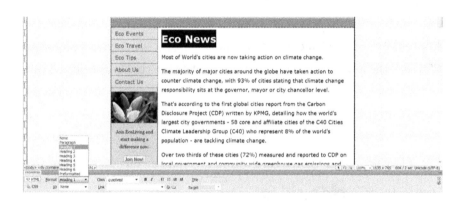

15 Click and drag to highlight the second line of text that starts with *Most of World's cities...* to format it as a subheading.

16 In the Properties panel, choose Heading 2 from the Format drop-down menu.

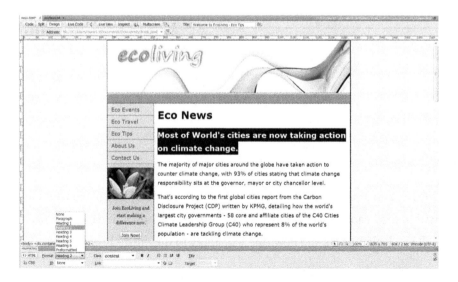

The heading looks quite big and because the subheading is long, it spreads over two lines. You're going to customise the headings using CSS. And you're going to create your own rule for the heading! Before you create a new CSS rule, you need to decide where you're going to position it within your stylesheet. To keep all the rules in a logical order (and easier to find later on), you're going to create new rules for headings directly below the existing rule for all headings (rule *h1, h2, h3, h4, h5, h6, p*). When you create a new CSS rule, the new rule is created directly below the currently selected rule.

17 Select **h1, h2, h3, h4, h5, h6, p** rule in the CSS Styles panel.

18 Place your cursor anywhere within the first heading on the page and click on the New CSS Rule button at the bottom of the CSS Styles panel (circled in red).

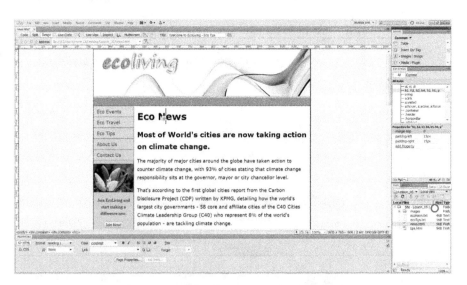

NOTE: You don't have to highlight the entire heading, just place your cursor within the heading. Because headings occupy their own line (they're what we call block elements), the new rule will apply to the entire line.

New CSS Rule dialogue box opens, and because you positioned your cursor within the heading 1 on the page, Dreamweaver sets the Selector Name to **.container .content h1** (h1 being the heading).

The **.container .content h1** rule means that new rule you are creating will apply to every heading 1 inside the rule called content (the right column on the page) inside the rule called container (the entire web page). This rule is far too specific, so you're going to shorten it a bit.

Click **Less Specific** button to change Selector Name to **.content h1**.

Now the rule still applies to heading 1 in the right column, but it's shorter.

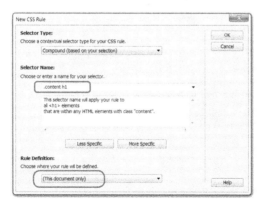

135

21 Keep **Selector Type** set to: **Compound**, and **Rule Definition** to:

This document only.

As described inside the New CSS Rule dialogue box, Compound selector type will create a new CSS rule based on your selection. Setting Rule Definition to: This document only will create a new CSS rule within the html document. Later on, you will be creating external stylesheets, but for now leave it the way it is.

22 Click OK and the CSS Rule Definition dialogue box will open. Now you can start customising the main heading.

23 Select Type category on the left and change the size of the text by typing 30 next to Font-size drop-down menu. If px doesn't display next to it, click on the drop-down menu and choose px. This will set the size of the heading to 30 pixels. Click Apply.

24 Click on the colour swatch next to **Color** property and in the drop-down menu that appears choose a dark green colour.

25 Click Apply to see the change.

26 Now, change the font for the heading. Select **Georgia, Times New Roman, Times, serif** font from the Font-family drop-down menu. Click Apply to notice the change.

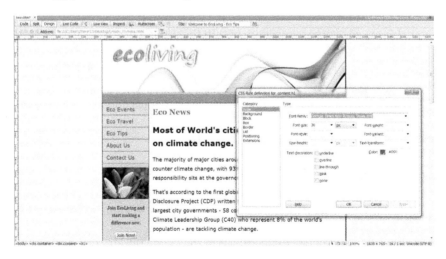

27 Finally, you'll change the text to italic. In the **Font-style** drop-down menu choose **italic**. Click OK.

Congratulations! You have successfully created a new CSS rule for the main heading and customised it! Well done. Now, the heading should look like on the screenshot below.

Now, you'll customise the subheading.

28 Place your cursor anywhere within the second heading on the page and click on the New CSS Rule button at the bottom of the CSS Styles panel.

29 New CSS Rule dialogue box opens, and because you positioned your cursor within the heading 2 on the page, Dreamweaver sets the Selector Name to **.container .content h2** (h2 being the heading).

30 Click **Less Specific** button to change Selector Name to **.content h2**. Now the rule still applies to heading 2 in the right column, but it's shorter.

138

31 Keep **Selector Type** set to: **Compound**, and **Rule Definition** to: **This document only**. Click OK.

32 Select Type category on the left and change the size of the text by typing 24 next to Font-size drop-down menu. If px doesn't display next to it, click on the drop-down menu and choose px. This will set the size of the heading to 24 pixels. Click Apply.

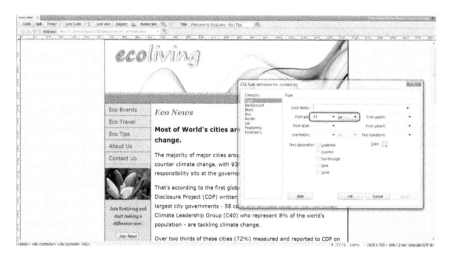

139

33 It's still too big. Change the size of the heading to 20px and click Apply.

34 Change the size of the heading to 19px and click OK.

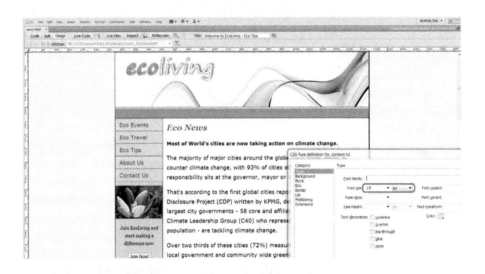

There are two more subheadings on this page. Because they have the same semantic meaning (they are the titles of the articles), you will define them as headings 2 as well. And because you have created rules for headings 2, the headings you will define in the next few steps will automatically inherit the same properties (19px size).

35 Scroll down the page and find line that reads **Dutch study shows**...
Place the cursor anywhere within this line on the page and in the Properties panel click on the drop-down menu next to **Format**. Choose **Heading 2**.

The text becomes a subheading with the same properties as the previous subheading near the top of the page.

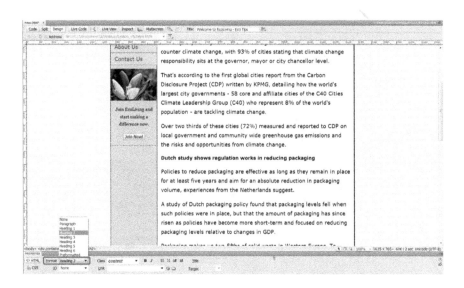

Scroll down the page to find another line for the subheading.

36 Find a line that reads **UN study shows 80%**... Place the cursor anywhere within this line on the page and in the Properties panel click on the drop-down menu next to **Format**. Choose **Heading 2**.

Fantastic! You have accomplished another task. You have defined the subheadings and customised them. It's time to see what the page looks like in the web browser and save it at the same time. Because Dreamweaver will prompt you to save the page when you try to preview it in a web browser, you're going to preview the page instead of saving it first and then previewing it.

37 Preview the page in a web browser by clicking on the browser icon at the top of the document window and selecting one of the web browsers on your system.

141

38 When prompted to save the change, click **Yes**.

39 When done previewing the page, close the web browser and close the

web page back in Dreamweaver. You're done with news.html.

142

Create Ordered and Unordered Lists

Text should be formatted to give it some meaning, and that's the reason behind using text formatting like lists. Lists are easier to read than blocks of text. In this exercise, you will use lists to display a number of ideas on saving the planet and living a more ecological life at home and at work.

40 Open **tips.html** and notice the image on the right side of the page in the right column. Leave it here for now.

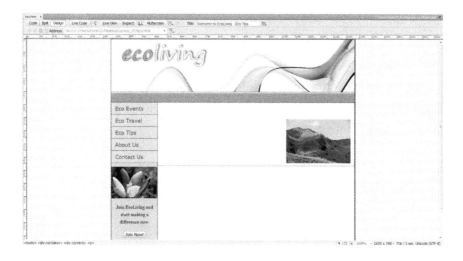

41 Double-click on **ecoTips.txt** file in the Files panel so it opens in Dreamweaver.

42 Highlight the entire text inside **ecoTips.txt** and copy it to the clipboard (Ctrl+C on Windows, Cmd+C on Mac). The text that appears within this text file shows on the screenshot on the next page.

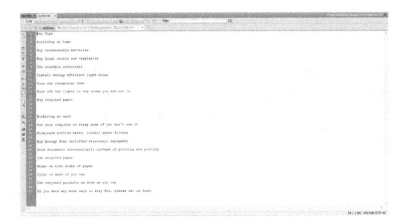

43 Close **ecoTips.txt**.

Now the tricky part. You want to insert all this text so that it wraps around
the image that appears on the right. For the text to wrap around the image,
it needs to be inserted after the image. The tricky part is how to place the
cursor after the image? Here's how:

44 Back to the page, **tips.html**, click on the image to highlight it.

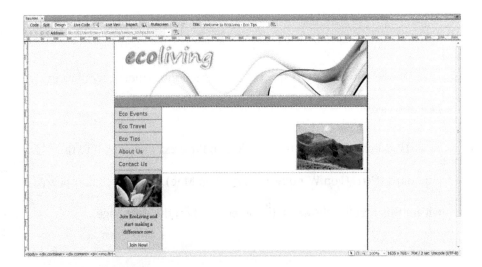

144

45 Press Right Arrow key on your keyboard to move cursor after image.

46 Paste the text you have copied to the clipboard by pressing Ctrl + V on Windows or Cmd + V on Mac.

47 If you can see a gap near the top of the page (as on the screenshot below), place your cursor inside this gap and press Delete key. This should fix the gap.

The text you have just inserted on the page will become an unordered list.

48 Highlight all text from the line that reads **Buy rechargeable batteries** to **Buy recycled paper**.

49 Navigate to the Properties panel and click on the Unordered List button as indicated on the screenshot below.

You can customise the list elements as either bullets or squares. The list you have just created does not use any graphics, it's a pure HTML list which makes it search engine friendly and quick to render in a web browser.

50 If you want to customise the list start by placing your cursor anywhere within the list.

51 Choose **Format > List > Properties...**

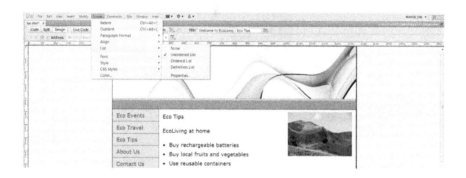

52 In the dialogue box that opens you can choose between **Bullet** and **Square** from the **Style** drop-down menu. Leave it on Default (Bullet) and click OK.

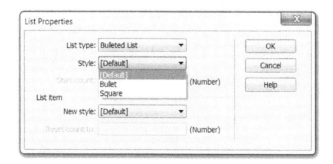

53 Scroll the page down to the next section below **EcoLiving at work** and highlight all the text from the line that reads **Put your computer...** to the bottom of the page.

54 Navigate to the Properties panel and click on the Unordered List button as indicated on the screenshot below.

55 If you want to use an ordered list instead, click on the icon next to it with your cursor within the list as indicated on the screenshot below.

For now just leave it as an unordered list. It makes more sense to format it as an unordered list as this list doesn't provide any logical steps or order.

148

Now it's time you customised the headings. There are three headings on this page - one main heading (the name of the page) and two sub-headings (names of the sections belonging to the lists). You'll use heading 1 for the main heading and heading 3 for the sub-headings.

56 Place your cursor in the first line that reads **Eco Tips** and format it as heading 1 by choosing **Heading 1** from the **Format** drop-down menu in the Properties panel.

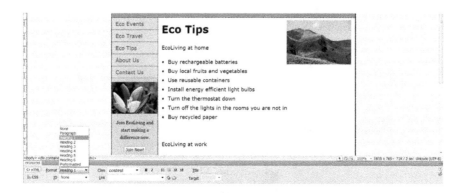

57 Place your cursor in the line that reads **EcoLiving at home** and format it as heading 3 by choosing **Heading 3** from the **Format** drop-down menu in the Properties panel.

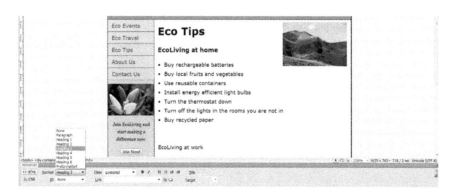

149

Heading 3 is a better choice than heading2 here as it is smaller. Even heading 3 is still a bit too big, so you're going to customise it now with CSS.

58 Navigate to the CSS Styles panel and select a rule **.content** (left screenshot). You're going to create a new CSS rule directly below. Place your cursor inside heading 3 on the page and click on the New CSS Rule icon in the CSS Styles panel(right screenshot).

59 In New CSS Rule dialogue box, leave Selector Type set to **Compound** and under Selector Name click **Less Specific** once so that name changes to **.content h3**. Rule Definition should say **(This document only)**. Click OK.

60 Select Type category and set Font-size property to **20px**. Change colour of the text by clicking on colour swatch next to Color property. Select dark green to match the colour scheme of the web page. Click OK.

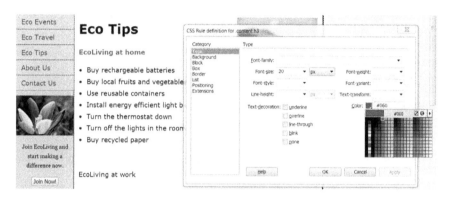

61 The next step will be to apply the same heading 3 to another section on the page. Place your cursor in the line that reads **EcoLiving at work** and change the Format in the Properties panel to **Heading 3**.

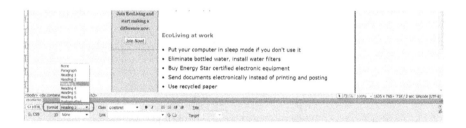

Now the headings for both lists look the same. Using CSS styles brings consistency in your designs. Every heading 3 on a page will look the same which is a purpose of the headings for articles/posts. And if you want to change the colour or text, you can quickly change it on every heading by simply altering the CSS rule **.content h3**.

62 Save and close tips.html.

Indenting Text Techniques

There are a few techniques for indenting text. Indenting text on web pages is a bit different from desktop applications and not as easy to apply. When indenting text on web pages, we need to think what would be the best way to achieve the effect and so it is web standards compliant.

An easy way to indent text is to use <blockquote> element, but to comply with all web standards, you should use custom CSS classes.

63 Open news.html. You're going to indent the articles that appear under the headings.

You're going to create a custom CSS class first and then you'll apply it to paragraphs of text.

64 Navigate to the CSS Styles panel and select the last rule **.clearfloat**.

65 Create New CSS Rule by clicking on the little page icon at the bottom of the CSS Styles panel.

66 Set the Selector Type to **Class** and in the Selector Name type **indentedText**. Click OK.

67 Select the Box category. Deselect Same for all under Margin and enter **30px** in the Right and Left margins.

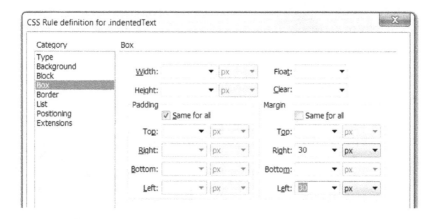

68 Select the Border category. Under Style select **ridge**, under Color select dark green colour, and under Width deselect Same for all and enter **1px** for Top and Left, **3px** for Right and Bottom. Click OK.

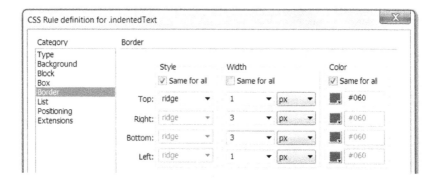

Now, you'll need to use the code a bit as well, so it would be best to work in Code view or Split view. Split view is easier to use so you'll use Split view so you could see the code and the design view at the same time.

69 Click on Split view button to display both code and design views at the same time.

NOTE: It's not important whether the code and design views display horizontally or vertically and which one appears on the left/right or bottom/top as long as you can see both the code and design views.

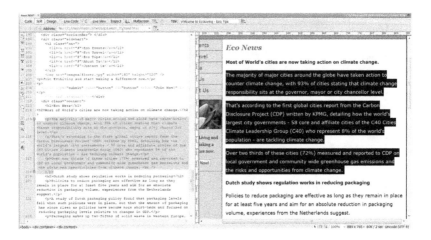

70 You need to highlight the entire three paragraphs in design view as on the screenshot above. Now look carefully at the code and see if the opening and closing <p> tags are included. If they're not, click and drag to highlight all the code indicated on the screenshot below.

```
214  <h2>Most of World's cities are now taking action on climate change.</h2
     >
215  <p>The majority of major cities around the globe have taken action
     to counter climate change, with 93% of cities stating that climate
     change responsibility sits at the governor, mayor or city chancellor
     level.</p>
216  <p>That's according to the first global cities report from the
     Carbon Disclosure Project (CDP) written by KPMG, detailing how the
     world's largest city governments - 58 core and affiliate cities of the
     C40 Cities Climate Leadership Group (C40) who represent 8% of the
     world's population - are tackling climate change.</p>
217  <p>Over two thirds of these cities (72%) measured and reported to
     CDP on local government and community wide greenhouse gas emissions and
     the risks and opportunities from climate change. <br />
218      </p>
```

71. With the code highlighted, click on the **Class** drop-down menu in the Properties panel and select **indentedText** class.

The text will now be indented and have a border around it. There is one more thing we need to change here - you now have three boxes instead of one! That's because there are three paragraphs here.

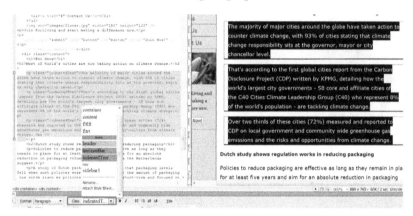

72. Go back to Design view by clicking on Design view button.

Place your cursor at the beginning of the second paragraph and press Backspace key on your keyboard so that the cursor moves to the line above as on the screenshot below.

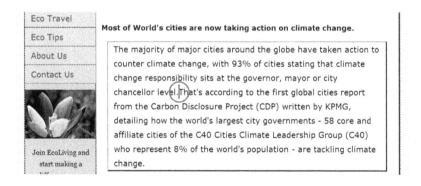

73 Press Shift+Enter twice to move cursor to next line and add line of text.

What you have just done is add a line break (or actually two) instead of creating paragraphs. And the text is nicely kept inside the box you have created in previous steps. Now you'll deal with the other paragraph.

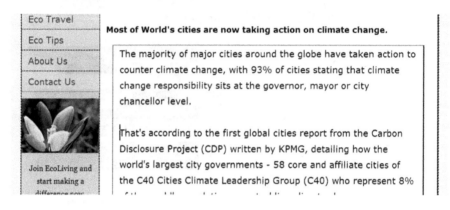

74 Place your cursor at the beginning of the last paragraph in this section and press Backspace key on your keyboard so that the cursor moves to the line above. Then press Shift + Enter twice as before so that all the text fits nicely inside the class you have created as on the screenshot below.

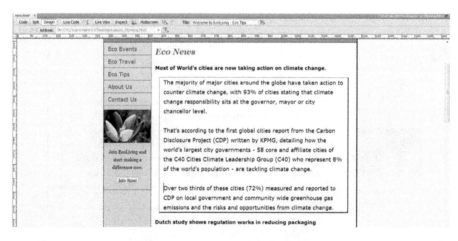

75 Preview the page in a web browser and save it when prompted.

76 Back to Dreamweaver move to the next article and follow steps 69 to 74. When you're done the second article should look like on the screenshot below.

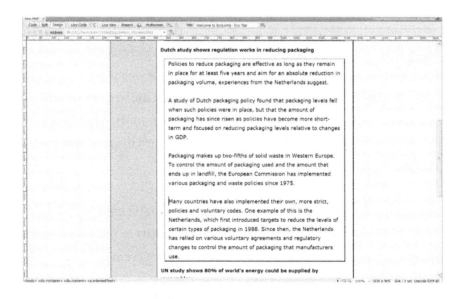

77 Finish the page by following the same steps 69 to 74 with the last paragraph so it looks like on the screenshot below.

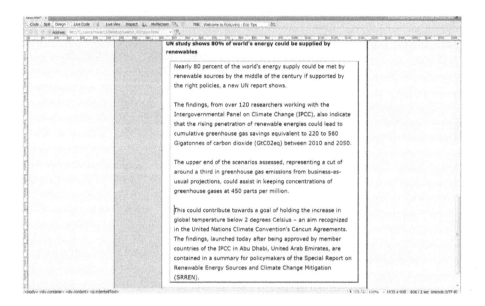

Tables

In the past, before the CSS was born, tables were widely used for page layout. Since CSS became powerful and a default choice for web pages layouts, we stopped using tables for layout purposes. Don't get me wrong - we still use tables. But not for layout purposes. Building page layouts with tables is a bad practise and has many disadvantages: tables are hard to create and format. They're also hard to edit.

So, although tables are bad for page design, they're still used to display data. Tables are good to display data like product lists or price lists. In this exercise you're going to use tables to display a list of events.

78 Open news.html if you closed it.

79 Using Split view scroll to bottom of the page and place cursor in the code view after the last paragraph. Press Enter to move to the next line.

80 Choose Insert > Table to insert a table on the page.

81 In the Table dialogue box enter 3 for Rows, 4 for Columns, 700px for Table width, 1 for Border thickness, and set the Header to Top by clicking on Top. Press OK.

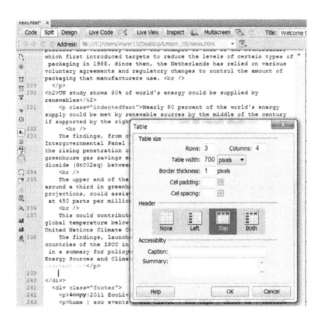

82 Click on Design view button to see newly created table on the page.

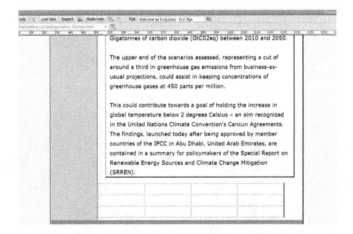

It's time to customise it. First, you're going to centre the table on the page using CSS. In the past, you would highlight the table on the page and aligned it to the centre using Properties panel (HTML), but as you already know, nowadays we're using CSS instead. To keep all the CSS rules in order, you will create a new CSS rule for a table under the **.content** rule. That's because the table is placed inside the div tag called content.

83 In the CSS Styles panel select the rule **.content**.

84 Place your cursor anywhere inside the table and using the Tag Inspector in the bottom left corner of the document window click on <table> tag to select the entire table.

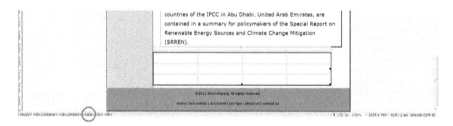

85 Create a new CSS rule in the CSS Styles panel. Set Selector Type to **Compound**, Selector Name to **.content table** (just click once on Less Specific), Rule Definition to **(This document only)** and click OK.

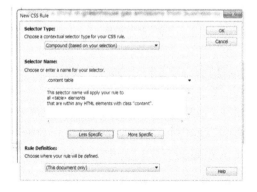

161

86 In the CSS Rule dialogue box select **Box** category, deselect Same for all for **Margin**, and choose **auto** for Right and Left. Click OK.

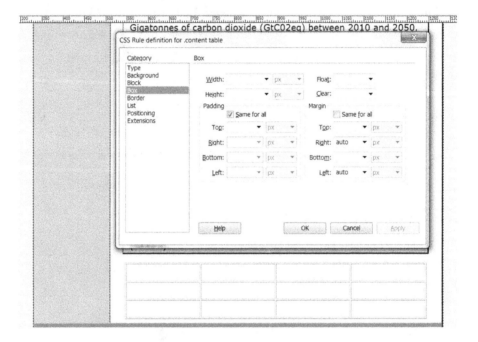

87 Now the table is centred on the page. Add some content. Type the content from the screenshot below:

As you start typing the content, you'll notice that the first row in the table gets bold and centred. That's because you've defined the first row to be a header and header by default is bold and centred. Leave it like that for now

162

and you're going to do a lot of customising this table in the future lesson when you get deeper into CSS.

88 Just before you finish, add some more content to the table.

Place your cursor in the last cell in the table and press Tab key on your keyboard. This will add a new row below.

89 Start adding the content from the screenshot below to add three additional rows in the table.

Date	Event	Location	Cost
Jan 1st	New Year's Parade	Central Park	Free
Jan 22nd	Chinese New Year	Central Market	Free
Feb 3rd	East Trail Tour	East Side	£10
Feb 25th	South Bank Festival	South Bank	Free
March 1st	Tower Bridge Tour	Tower Bridge	£10

90 Preview the page in a web browser and save it at the same time as prompted by Dreamweaver.

You're going to finish this lesson by adding some space above and below the table. Using CSS of course.

92 Select the **.content table** rule in the CSS Styles panel and edit it.

93 Select **Box** category and enter the values of **30px** for **Margin** Top and Bottom as indicated on the screenshot on the next page.

94 Accept the changes by pressing OK.

95 Save and preview the page in a web browser. That's your final result.

Congratulations! You have successfully finished Lesson 5.

Review Questions

1. What HTML elements occupy their own line on a page?

2. What text file formats can Dreamweaver open?

3. What happens when you try to open .rtf file in Dreamweaver?

4. What's the reason for using Lists on the web pages?

Review Answers

1. Block elements occupy their own line on a page. An example of a block element is a heading i.e. h1, h2, h3 etc

2. Dreamweaver can open .txt files.

3. As Dreamweaver doesn't open .rtf files, the file will open in your default text editor for .rtf files, i.e. WordPad on Windows.

4. Text should be formatted to give it some meaning, and that's the reason behind using text formatting like lists. Lists are easier to read than blocks of text.

Lesson 6

Images

In this lesson you're going to start working with images and learn how to:

- Differentiate File Formats

- Add Images to the web pages

- Use Assets panel

- Import images using Adobe Bridge

- Import images from Photoshop and Fireworks

- Use Photoshop Smart Objects

- Edit images with Dreamweaver and Fireworks

This lesson will take about 1 hour 15 minutes to complete.

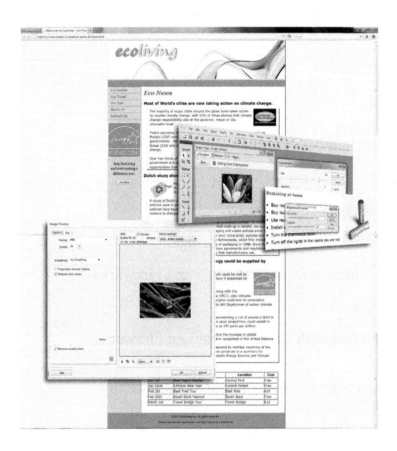

Basics of Images on the web

Images are essential on the web. They bring life to web pages. All web pages use images.

There are two main categories of graphics or images:
- vector graphics
- raster graphics

Before we jump into describing vector and raster graphics, let me share with you a bit of information about imagery on the screens.
Computer displays are composed of a number of small cells - rectangles called pixels and the image on the screen is built from these cells.

Vector graphics are created using mathematical calculations, which allows for resizing images without losing the quality. However, because vector graphics are created with maths, they're mainly used for logos, line art and drawings. Vector graphics are basically a number of lines, shapes, and curves. Most logos are built with vector graphics. When creating a vector image, the mathematical formulas determine where to put the dots that create the image to get the best results when displaying the image. These formulas can produce an image that's scalable to any size with great quality.
Vector images are usually saved in these file formats:
- AI
- EPS
- PICT

However, the above three file formats are not supported by the web browsers, hence they're mostly used in vector applications like Adobe Illustrator, and then exported to SVG (Scalable Vector Graphic).

Raster graphics, or bitmap images as we call them, are composed from pixels - little, perfectly square dots of colour.

Raster images are much more popular on the web than vector graphics. Raster images are built from thousands and even millions of pixels that produce the final image. Each pixel within image has certain colour.

What mostly affects the quality of raster images, is the resolution. Resolution is a number of pixels within one inch. The more pixels per inch, the higher resolution of the image and the better the quality. Unfortunately, the higher the resolution the bigger the file size. Luckily, when you're building the websites, the images are only going to be displayed on screen and they don't need a higher resolution. The images on the screen are using a resolution of 72 ppi, so the file size will be much smaller if you compare with an image that is going to printed and uses a resolution of 300.

The screenshots below illustrate the quality of the image at the resolution of 300ppi (on the left) and 72ppi (on the right).

If you look carefully at the images, you'll notice that on the image on the right people are pixelated and so are the buildings. The buildings and people on the image on the left are all sharp and in focus.

Because one of the most important factors when building websites is the speed at which the page loads into a web browser, you'll be optimizing the images and the images will be much smaller than the entire web page.

170

Colour is another important factor when preparing images for the web. Screens (nowadays you need to bear in mind portable devices like mobile phones and tablets as well) display only a fraction of the colours that human eye can see. And they display different levels of colour:

- mobile phones usually support up to 65,000 colours (with more and more mobile phones displaying even more)
- computer screens support up to 16.7 millions of colours.

The more colours image contains, the bigger the file size. That's why you'll look for compromise between resolution, file size and colour to get optimal quality with small file size so images load quickly on a web page.

Differentiate File Formats

The most popular file formats on the web are: JPEG, PNG, and GIF. All of these file formats are compatible with all the web browsers.

GIF

GIF stands for **Graphics Interchange Format** and it was one of the first file formats created. GIF doesn't use lossy compression (as JPEG does), but instead it limits the file size by limiting number of colours in the image. GIF is limited to only 256 colours, so it's not well suited for photographs, as they contain gradients and soft edges and millions of colours. It is very popular for elements like:

- logos, illustrations, buttons, and web interfaces.

JPEG

JPEG stands for **J**oint **P**hotographic **E**xperts **G**roup and it is a file format that was created in 1992 to deal with the limitations of GIF file format. It reduces the file size by using the lossy compression. When you save a JPEG, you decide how much information you want to retain

171

in the image and the more information you retain (the higher the quality setting) the bigger the file size. Your aim would be to reduce the file size as much as possible while retaining good quality of the image without creating distortions.

JPEG is the most popular file format and one of its powerful features is support for unlimited resolution. That's why it is a default choice for images on the web and a default file format on most digital cameras as a way of storing images on a memory card.

One big disadvantage of JPEG file format is lack of support for transparency.

PNG

PNG stands for **P**ortable **N**etwork **G**raphic and it was created in 1995. PNG incorporates some of the best features of both GIF and JPEG:

- it supports transparency, unlimited resolution, and lossless compression.

Even though PNG has been around for a long time, its adoption wasn't fully implemented until recently as Internet Explorer 6 didn't support transparency in PNG files. PNG is also a great file format for saving screenshots and many scanners use PNG as their default fie format for saving scans.

Add Images to the web pages

1 Launch Adobe Dreamweaver CS5, if it is not already open.

2 If you see the Welcome Screen, click on Dreamweaver Site button to define a new Site. If you don't see the Welcome Screen (you may have disabled it through the Dreamweaver Properties), choose Site > New Site from the menu. The Site Setup dialogue box appears.

In the Site Name field, type **Lesson_06**.

In the Local Site Folder field, click on the folder icon to the right and navigate to the **Lesson_06** folder containing the files for this lesson.

Select **Lesson_06** folder, and click Open (Windows) or Choose (Mac). Then, click Select (Windows) or Choose (Mac) to choose this folder as your local root folder.

Click the arrow next to the **Advanced Settings** category on the left to reveal a list of tabs. Select **Local Info** category and next to **Default Images folder** field, click the folder icon. When the dialogue box opens, navigate to the images folder located inside Lesson_06 folder and click Select (Windows) or Choose (Mac).

In the Site Setup dialogue box click Save.

Here's the structure of Lesson 06 in Files panel:

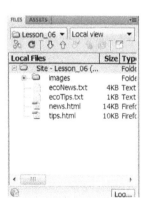

Choose File > Open, and select **news.html**.

When the page opens, select the flower image in the sidebar and delete it by pressing Delete key on your keyboard.

Now, you're going to insert a new image.

173

10 Choose Insert > Image. As Select Image Source dialogue box appears, navigate to the Lesson_06 folder and select **energyStar_logo.png**.

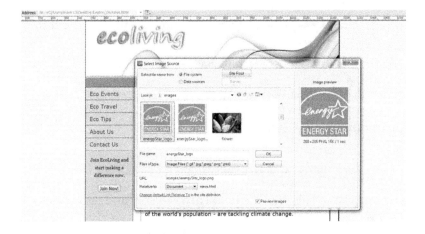

11 Press OK and in the Image Tag Accessibility Attributes dialogue box type **Energy Start logo**. Press OK.

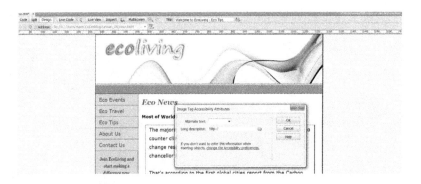

12 The image is a bit wider than the sidebar, so you're going to resize the image using some of the Dreamweaver tools.

Your web page should now look like on the screenshot on the next page.

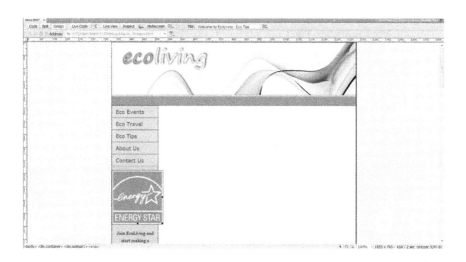

Sometimes you may need to perform some simple edits of the images quickly within Dreamweaver. Dreamweaver has built-in features that allow you to perform some of these tasks within Dreamweaver interface. In the next step, you're going to resize the image in the sidebar so it fits within the sidebar's width.

13   Select the image on the page if it's not already selected.

14   Look into the Properties panel as it now displays all the options for

the image. Among many options you'll notice here are the dimensions of the image on the left next to **W** and **H** properties.

The image is 200px wide while the sidebar is only 180px wide.

15 Change the image width to **180** and the height to **184**. Now the image fits nicely into the sidebar.

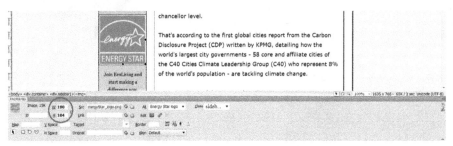

Now, you're going to insert images in the right column using different method for each image. You have used the Insert menu already, now it's time for the Insert panel.

Insert panel offers several categories that you can use to easily add images, media, and many more.

16 In Insert panel, click on the drop-down menu and choose **Common**.

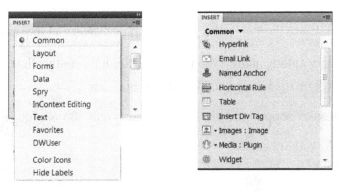

Common category in the Insert panel gives you quick access to the most often used elements on web pages. In this case, Common category gives you quick access to the button that inserts images on the web pages. Next to the Images button there is a down-pointing triangle, so there is a submenu here which will give you additional options.

176

17 Place your cursor at the beginning of the paragraph that starts with

The majority of major cities...

18 Navigate to the Insert panel and choose **Image** from the Images

drop-down menu in the Common category.

19 Select Image Source dialog box appears. Navigate to the images

folder and select **climateChange.gif**, and press OK (Choose on Mac).

20 Type **Climate change** in the Alternate text field in the Image Tag

Accessibility Attributes dialogue box and press OK.

The image should appear at the beginning of the paragraph as on the
screenshot on the next page. The next step will be to change its position
so it appears on the right and text flows around the image. You will
achieve it with a class that is included with the starter page that you used
to create this page.

2.1 Select the image on the page if it's not already selected and navigate to the Properties panel.

2.2 In the Properties panel choose **fltrt** from the Class drop-down menu as shown on the screenshot below.

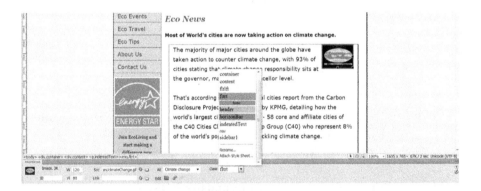

The image now nicely aligns with the right side of the column and the text is flowing around the image. In the next lesson you're going to customise the fltrt class to adjust how the image appears on the page. Now you're going to add another image in the next section of the page using another method. This time you're going to use the Assets panel.

178

Use Assets panel

Assets panel displays assets for the site associated with the document that is active in the Document window. That's why you will need to define a Dreamweaver site before using the Assets panel. Assets panel provides two ways of displaying assets as shown below:

Site list   **Favorites list**

- Site list shows all of the assets in your site (to access images, click on the first icon in the top left corner - icon that looks like a tree).
- Favorites list only shows assets that you have chosen, so it should be empty.

To access the Site list or the Favorites list, click on one of the buttons on the top of the Assets panel. By default, assets are listed alphabetically so it's easier to find them. If you prefer, you can change the sorting of images by clicking on one of the columns: Name, Dimensions, Size or Type.

Name	Dimensions	Size	Type
background.jpg	5x30	1KB	JPEG image
batteries.jpg	250x271	19KB	JPEG image
climateChange.gif	120x88	3KB	GIF image

179

23 Scroll the page down to the next article that starts with **Policies to reduce packaging**...

24 Navigate to the Assets panel and find the image **recycled_small.jpg**.

NOTE: If you don't see the Assets panel, choose Window > Assets.

25 Place your cursor at the beginning of the paragraph.

26 Select **recycled_small.jpg** in the Assets panel and click Insert button at the bottom of the panel.

27 Type **Recycling** in the Alternate text field in the Image Tag Accessibility Attributes dialogue box and press OK.

28 Select the image on the page if it's not already selected and navigate to the Properties panel.

29 Now align it to the left. In the Properties panel choose **fltlft** from the Class drop-down menu as shown on the screenshot on the next page.

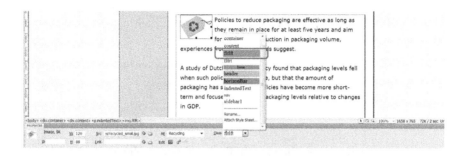

Now you're going to use another method for inserting images. This time you're going to drag and drop an image on the page and you will be using Assets panel for that.

30 Scroll the page down to the next article that starts with **Nearly 80 percent of the world's energy**...

31 Navigate to the Assets panel and find the image **energyStar_ logo_small.jpg**.

32 Click on the image to select it and holding the mouse button down start dragging it onto the page. As you start moving the image around, the cursor will appear on the page.

33 Move the image close to the beginning of the paragraph and when the cursor appears at the beginning of the paragraph release the mouse button.

34 Type **Energy Star logo** in the Alternate text field in the Image Tag Accessibility Attributes dialogue box and press OK.

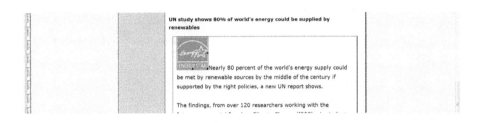

35 Select the image on the page if it's not already selected and navigate to the Properties panel.

36 Now align it to the right. In the Properties panel choose **fltrt** from the Class drop-down menu.

37 Preview the page in a web browser by clicking on the browser icon at the top of the document window and selecting one of the web browsers on your system.

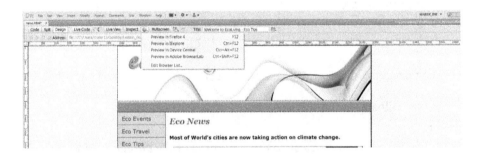

38 When prompted to save the change, click **Yes**.

On the next page you'll see the preview of the page in Mozilla Firefox.

39 When done previewing the page, close the web browser and close the web page back in Dreamweaver. You're done with news.html.

Import images using Adobe Bridge

Adobe Bridge is an essential application for web designers. It is a cross-platform file browser and you can use Adobe Bridge to quickly browse directories of images. It is fully integrated with Dreamweaver. You can launch Bridge straight from Dreamweaver to browse through the images before you drag them into your page.

NOTE: Adobe Bridge is only installed with Dreamweaver CS5 when you install Adobe Creative Suite CS5. It is NOT included in a standalone version of Dreamweaver CS5.

Now, you will use Bridge to drag and drop an image onto your web page.

183

40 Open **tips.html** and notice the image on the right side of the page in the right column.

41 Select the image on the right side and press Delete key on your keyboard to delete it.

42 Launch Adobe Bridge by choosing **File > Browse in Bridge...**

NOTE: You could just launch Bridge on its own from the list of applications (Applications on Mac and Program Files on Windows), but there is a reason why you are launching Bridge from Dreamweaver. Here's why:

If you launch Bridge from Dreamweaver, Bridge will automatically open and navigate into your site folder! How great is that? So now, you should have Bridge opened pointing to Lesson_06 folder as on the screenshot below:

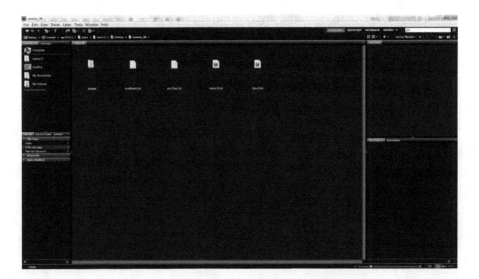

43 Double click images folder to open it. If the images thumbnails are small, resize them using slider in the bottom right corner of Bridge.

NOTE: To make sure you work with the same workspace and the arrangement of the panels is the same, make sure you are working in the **Essentials** workspace. You'll find the name of the workspace in the top right corner of the Bridge interface as shown on the screenshot here:

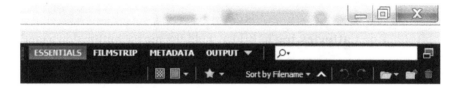

Bridge has a fantastic feature called Compact Mode. You're going to use it to insert an image on a page in Dreamweaver. What is exciting about the Compact Mode is that when you activate it Bridge interface gets smaller so you can see the other applications (and that's great because you want to see Dreamweaver), but it also stays on top of other applications! All the time! Very exciting feature in Dreamweaver.

44 To activate Compact Mode in Bridge click on the Compact Mode icon in the top right corner of the application window as shown here:

185

45 With Bridge and Dreamweaver visible (you can move Bridge to a side so you can see the Dreamweaver page clearly) find the image **batteries.jpg**.

46 Click on **batteries.jpg** in Bridge, hold the mouse button down, and drag it into Dreamweaver. When cursor appears at beginning of the line that reads **EcoLiving at home**, release the mouse button to insert the image.

47 Type **Rechargeable batteries** in the Alternate text field in the Image Tag Accessibility Attributes dialogue box and press OK.

Congratulations! You have successfully inserted an image using Bridge and its Compact Mode.

48 Close Adobe Bridge.

49 Select the image on the page if it's not already selected and navigate to the Properties panel.

50 Now align it to the right. In the Properties panel choose **fltrt** from the Class drop-down menu.

51 Preview the page in a web browser by clicking on the browser icon at the top of the document window and selecting one of the web browsers on your system.

52 When prompted to save the change, click **Yes**.

Here's the preview of the page in Internet Explorer.

Import images from Photoshop and Fireworks

Adobe Photoshop and Adobe Fireworks are both excellent applications used for editing and optimising graphics for the web. Usually you prepare graphic in one of these applications and export it as a GIF, PNG or JPG. However, you can also copy and paste images between Photoshop / Fireworks and Dreamweaver. In this exercise, you're going to use Adobe Photoshop.

53 Launch Adobe Photoshop. Choose **File > Open** and select **grass.jpg**.

54 Select the entire image by choosing **Select > All** or pressing **Ctrl + A** on Windows or **Cmd + A** on Mac.

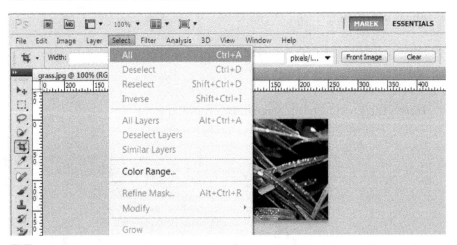

55 Copy the selected image into the clipboard by choosing **Edit > Copy** or pressing **Ctrl +C** on Windows or **Cmd + C** on Mac.

56 Navigate back to Dreamweaver. Place your cursor at the beginning of the paragraph that reads **EcoLiving at work**.

188

57 Paste the image by choosing **Edit > Paste** or pressing **Ctrl + V** on

Windows or **Cmd + V** on Mac.

58 Image Preview dialogue box should appear.

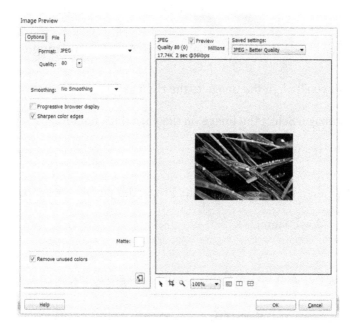

When you insert an image from Photoshop, the Image Preview dialogue box appears to allow you to adjust various settings to optimise the graphic. The Image Preview dialogue box has three main sections:

- Options tab - to define what file format you want to use
- File tab - to set the scale and target the file size
- Preview panel - to see the image in a file format defined in the Options tab.

The options depend on the file format you choose.

189

59 Set the Options tab to **JPEG** and Quality to **80**. Press OK.

60 Save Web Image dialogue box should appear because you need to save the file. Just click **Save**.

61 When Confirm Save As dialogue box appears just click **Yes**.

62 In the Image Description dialogue box type **Grass image**. Click OK.

63 Now you'll align the image to the right as you have done with the previous image. Select the image on the page if it's not already selected and navigate to the Properties panel.

64 Now align it to the right. In the Properties panel choose **fltrt** from the Class drop-down menu.

Both images appear on the right side of the page as shown on the screenshot.

65 Close Adobe Photoshop. If prompted to save any changes, click No.

The above technique in this exercise works in the same way in both Adobe Photoshop and Adobe Fireworks. In this exercise you used Photoshop and in the later exercise on editing images you're going to use Fireworks. If you want to try to use Fireworks instead of Photoshop, follow steps 53 - 59 in Fireworks.

Use Photoshop Smart Objects

Dreamweaver supports Photoshop Smart Objects, which means you can add a PSD file to your web page and optimise it for the web. PSD is a native file format in Photoshop with support for layers and effects, but it doesn't display in the web browsers so Dreamweaver is going to save it to one of the supported file formats (GIF, PNG or JPG). However, when you save a Smart Object to one of these file formats Dreamweaver will keep a live connection to the original PSD file. This is the workflow for PSD files that Adobe recommends. If you make any changes to the PSD file, a red arrow will appear on the image on your web page in Dreamweaver to let you know that the original file has changed.

Image in Sync

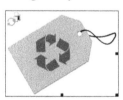

Image out of Sync

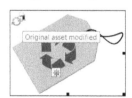

191

In this part of the lesson you're going to replace the image **grass.jpg** with image with a recycling logo on it and you will import it as a Smart Object.

66 Back to Dreamweaver, you should still have **tips.html** open. If not, open it from the Lesson_06 folder.

67 Select **grass.jpg** image on the right side of the page and press Delete key on your keyboard to delete it.

Now you're going to insert a PSD file. You have used a number of different ways of inserting images in the previous exercises in this lesson. You used:
◦ Insert menu
◦ Insert panel
◦ Assets panel
This time you're going to use the Files panel just to give you another option, so you can decide which one you like most.

68 Navigate to the Files panel and double click on the images folder to open it as on the right screenshot below.

The file you're looking for is **recycled.psd**. This is the file you're going to add to the page as the next step.

69 Select **recycled.psd** in the Files panel. Click on the image to select it and holding the mouse button down start dragging it onto the page. As you start moving the image around, the cursor will appear on the page.

70 Move the image close to the beginning of the paragraph that reads **EcoLiving at work** and when the cursor appears at the beginning of this paragraph release the mouse button.

71 Image Preview dialogue box should appear.

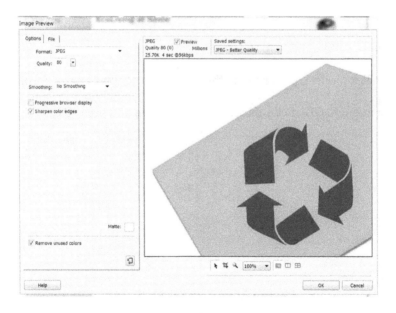

In this step you're going to resize the image and optimise it before you save it (remember that the web browsers do not display PSD files).

72 In the Image Preview dialogue box click on the File tab in the top left corner, set **Scale W** (Width) to **250** and press Tab key on your keyboard. H (Height) will automatically change to 184px.

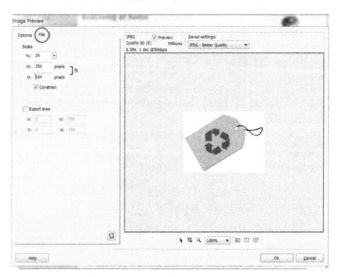

73 Click on the Options tab in the top left corner and set the Format drop-down menu to GIF. Set number of colours to **64** and press **OK**.

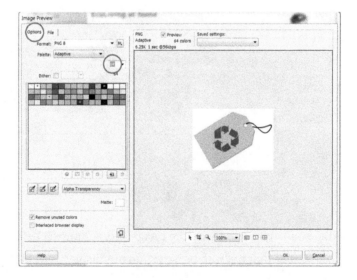

74 When Save Web Image dialogue box appears, save it as recycled.png and click Save.

75 Type **Recycling logo** in the Alternate text field in the Image Tag Accessibility Attributes dialogue box and press OK.

76 Now align the image to the right. In the Properties panel choose **fltrt** from the Class drop-down menu..

77 Preview the page in a web browser and save it when prompted.

78 Back to Dreamweaver notice the icon that appears in the top left corner of the image. This icon identifies that this image is a Smart Object.

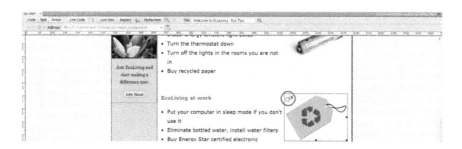

The green circular arrows indicate that the original image is the same as the image placed on the page. If you change the original image, the arrows will change and you'll see it in just a moment. You'll change the original file outside Dreamweaver. You're going to colourise it a bit.

79 Launch Adobe Photoshop. Choose **File > Open** and select **recycled.psd**.

195

80 In Photoshop, choose **Image > Adjustments > Hue/Saturation**.

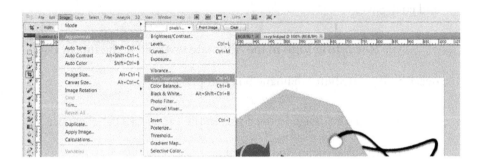

81 In the Dialogue box that opens, move the Saturation slider to **+30** to shift the colour in the image and press OK.

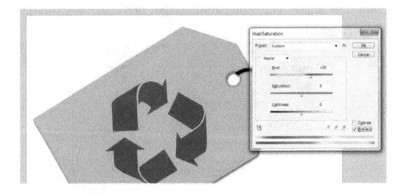

82 Save the file by choosing **File > Save** or pressing **Ctrl+S** on Windows or **Cmd+S** on Mac and close Photoshop.

83 Back to Dreamweaver, notice how the icon on the image changed.

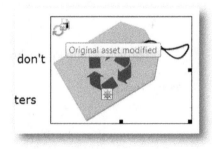

196

Dreamweaver indicates that the original file has changed. You don't have to update the file now. You can do it later on. So how do you update the image? It's really simple.

84 Right-click image and choose **Update from Original** in menu.

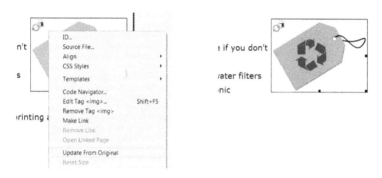

The image has updated. As you can see, Photoshop Smart Objects are great in designing process. They're perfect for images that are often updated.

Edit images with Dreamweaver and Fireworks

One of the most important factors when preparing images for the web is to optimise them, in other words, to balance the quality of the image with pixel dimensions and file size. When preparing images that go on the web page, you would use a graphics editor i.e. Adobe Photoshop or Adobe Fireworks. But what if you want to edit an image that's already been placed on the page? Dreamweaver offers some features that you can use to modify an existing image without having to use an external graphics editor. You are limited however to what you can do in Dreamweaver as you're going to see in just a moment. It all comes down to what you

197

need to change, in some cases Dreamweaver editing features will be enough. You're going to start by inspecting what Dreamweaver can do first before moving to Fireworks.

85 Scroll to the top of the page and select **batteries.jpg**. Inspect the Properties panel in detail.

Starting from the left, you'll find:
- the file size in the top left corner (Image, 19K),
- below the file size a field called ID - we'll talk about it in the future lesson on navigation,
- the dimensions of the image (**W** and **H**),
- moving to the right **Src** field - location of the file (images/batteries.jpg),
- directly below - link field (more on that in the lesson on navigation),
- Alt field for Alternative Text for Accessibility,
- and finally Edit section below:

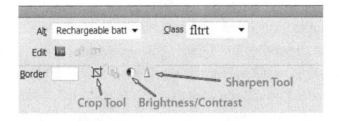

NOTE: For now, don't worry if the icon next to the word Edit has Ps instead of Fw on it.

Here's the explanation of the icons:

○ Crop Tool - you can use this tool to crop the image, bear in mind that the original image will change on the hard drive.

○ Brightness/Contrast - adjusting brightness or contrast of the pixels in an image. You would use it if the image is too bright or too dark.

○ Sharpen Tool - increasing sharpness by increasing the contrast of pixels around the edges of the object.

NOTE: These tools change the original image on the hard drive and when trying to use them, Dreamweaver warns you by displaying this message:

In the next step, you're going to darken batteries.jpg a bit.

86 With **batteries.jpg** selected, click on **Brightness/Contrast** icon.

87 When the warning dialogue box appears just press OK.

88 In the dialogue box that appears move both sliders as indicated on the screenshot below to darken the image a bit and to reduce contrast.

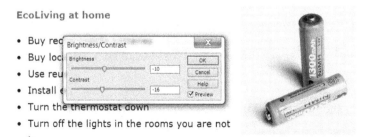

89 Press OK to accept the changes.

Congratulations! You have just adjusted the image within Dreamweaver!
Well done. Now, you're going to use Fireworks to edit another image as the
last exercise in this lesson.

90 Open Dreamweaver Preferences to define Fireworks as your default

image editor. On Windows **Edit > Preferences**, on Mac **Dreamweaver >**

Preferences.

91 Select **File Types / Editors** category on the left and on the right select

.jpg .jpe .jpeg in the Extensions column as indicated below.

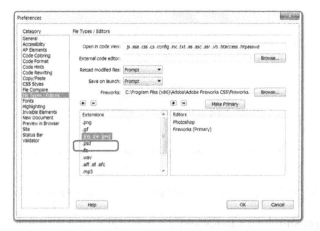

92 In the right column (Editors) select **Fireworks** and click on **Make**

Primary button above the column. Press OK to go back to Dreamweaver.

Now you should see the Fireworks icon in the Properties panel when you
select **flower.jpg** in the sidebar on the left.

93 Select **flower.jpg** in the sidebar on the left and click on Fireworks

icon (Fw) in the Properties panel to edit the image with Fireworks. Notice

that you don't have to start Fireworks first, Dreamweaver will do it for

you as on the screenshot below.

94 When Fireworks starts, you will see this message:

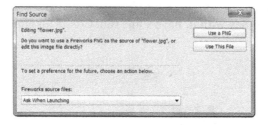

Fireworks has its own native file format called Fireworks PNG, which

supports layers, pages, and layer effects - similar to Photoshop's PSD or

Illustrator's AI, and here Fireworks wants to know if you have created the

image of the flower from a Fireworks PNG file. This file was created in

Photoshop, so there is no Fireworks PNG file.

95 Click **Use This File** and the image will open inside Fireworks.

There is one big difference between editing images with Photoshop and Fireworks from Dreamweaver. Fireworks was designed to work with Dreamweaver and has a closer integration. Look at the top of the document window in Fireworks:

It says: **Editing from Dreamweaver** and there's a **Done** button next to it. That's what we call Roundtrip Editing, you won't see this message in Photoshop. I'm not saying you cannot edit images with Photoshop - of course you can. I'm just saying it is easier and faster to do it with Fireworks.

97 Choose **Filters > Adjust Color > Hue/Saturation** to colourise

image.

98 In dialogue box that appears move the Hue slider to shift the colours in

the image. Just play with it, have some fun. Create an effect you like. Click OK

99 Click **Done** at top of document window to go back to Dreamweaver.

Notice how Fireworks automatically redirects you back to Dreamweaver and the image updates! That's how you edit images with Fireworks.

Congratulations! You have successfully finished Lesson 6.

202

Review Questions

1. How are the vector graphics created?

2. What happens when you try to insert an image from Photoshop into Dreamweaver' page?

3. How can you access the Site list of the Favorites list in the Assets panel?

4. What web file formats support transparency?

Review Answers

1. Vector graphics are created using mathematical calculations, which allows for resizing images without losing the quality

2. When you insert an image from Photoshop into Dreamweaver' page, the Image Preview dialogue box appears to allow you to adjust various settings to optimise the image.

3. To access the Site list or the Favorites list, click on one of the buttons on the top of the Assets panel.

4. PNG and GIF file formats support transparency.

Lesson 7

Navigation

In this lesson you're going to start working with navigation and learn how to:

- Create internal links

- Create links to external websites

- Create links to images

- Set up e-mail links

- Insert drop-down menu

- Customise drop-down menu with CSS

This lesson will take about 1 hour 30 minutes to complete.

Basics of Hyperlinks

If we didn't have hyperlinks, the Web would be a totally different experience. Can you imagine browsing the internet without hyperlinks? Let's say you want to navigate from one website to another and as there are no hyperlinks, you need to type a new web address in a web browser address bar instead of just clicking on a link on a page. My guess is the Web would be a boring place as it would take you so much time browsing through the web pages.

What are Hyperlinks you may be asking? Hyperlink, or link as we usually call it as it's shorter, is an element on a page that has a connection with another element on the same computer or on the Internet.

Here's how the World Wide Web Consortium define a link:

A hyperlink (or link) is a word, group of words, or image that you can click on to jump to a new document or a new section within the current document.

When you move the cursor over a link in a Web page, the arrow will turn into a little hand.

Links are specified in HTML using the <a> tag. The behaviour of the hyperlink is specified by HTML, as in the example below:

```
<a href="http://www.saitraining.co.uk/training.
html" target="_blank"> Sai Training - Adobe Certified
Training </a>
```

Here's a quick overview of the code:

○ **a** is an HTML element that defines a link

○ **href** is an attribute that points to page or file (in this case a web page)

○ the address of a web page or a file that is going to load upon click follows the href attribute and appears in quotes

○ **target** attribute defines whether the link is going to open in a new tab/ window or is going to reload the content within the same window, we'll talk about it later in this lesson

○ after the > symbol comes a text that is going to be visible to the visitor

○ finally, the closing tag **</a>** defines the end of the link

Here's an example that shows what the link looks like on a web page and how the cursor changes when positioned over the link:

Internal or External links?

Both kinds of links, internal and external, work in a very similar way - they are defined in HTML code by the <a> tag.

Internal links take the visitor to another page or file (to be downloaded) within the same website.

External links take the visitor to another website on the Internet or to a file (to be downloaded) from another website.

Create internal links

Creating links in Dreamweaver is very easy as you're going to see in just a moment. In this part of the lesson, you're going to create text based menu and create links between the pages. You're going to use different techniques to create links between the pages.

1. Launch Adobe Dreamweaver CS5, if it is not already open.

2. If you see the Welcome Screen, click on Dreamweaver Site button to define a new Site. If you don't see the Welcome Screen (you may have disabled it through the Dreamweaver Properties), choose Site > New Site from the menu. The Site Setup dialogue box appears.

3. In the Site Name field, type **Lesson_07**.

4. In the Local Site Folder field, click on the folder icon to the right and navigate to the **Lesson_07** folder containing the files for this lesson.

5. Select **Lesson_07** folder, and click Open (Windows) or Choose (Mac). Then, click Select (Windows) or Choose (Mac) to choose this folder as your local root folder.

6. Click arrow next to the **Advanced Settings** category on the left to reveal tabs. Select **Local Info** category and next to **Default Images folder** field, click the folder icon. When dialogue box opens, go to images folder inside Lesson_07 and click Select(Windows) or Choose(Mac).

7 In the Site Setup dialogue box click Save.

Here's the structure of Lesson 07 in Files panel:

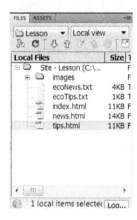

8 Choose File > Open, and select **index.html**.

9 When the page opens, place your cursor in the horizontal section directly below the header. That's where you're going to create a text based menu.

NOTE: If you find it hard to place your cursor in the designated area, go to **Step 10**.

10 Open the document in Split view so you can see both Design and Code view as indicated on the screenshot below.

11 Place your cursor between horizonBar class tags as shown on the screenshot below.

12 Type the word Home and click on the Design View button to navigate to the Design View. The word Home should appear on the page.

13 Place your cursor after the word Home, press **Spacebar** once and type | **Eco News | Eco Tips**.

NOTE: You will find a vertical line, also called Pipe in programming languages, on your keyboard. You may need to hold the Shift key at the same time when pressing the Pipe symbol on the keyboard.
The Pipe symbol is often used to seperate menu elements without using any graphics. Make sure you add spaces between Pipes and text as indicated.

211

14 Your menu should now look like this:

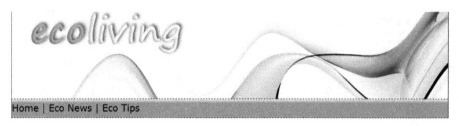

In the next step you're going to change the position of the menu with some CSS so it appears on the right and aligns to the right as well.

15 Go to the CSS Styles panel and select **.horizonBar** rule. Click on the pencil icon to edit the rule.

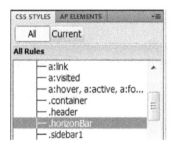
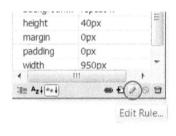

16 In the CSS Rule Definition dialogue box that opens, make the following changes: in **Block** category set **Text-align** to **right**, in **Type** category set **Color** property to a bright colour (yellow for example), and set **Font-size** to **85%**. Press OK.

17 Your menu should now be nicely aligned to the right of the page and the font should be a bit smaller than the rest of the text on the page (85% of the original).

Now you're going to start adding links to the pages using the menu you have just created.

18 Highlight the word **Home** in the horizontal menu section and choose **Insert > Hyperlink**. In the dialogue box that appears leave the Text as Home and in the **Link** section below type #. For **Target** click on the drop-down menu next to it and choose **_self**. Click OK.

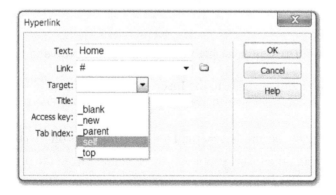

Hash (#) symbol creates a so-called "dummy link" - a link that doesn't link to anywhere but allows you to check the link interaction, so you can see your cursor changing to a hand icon when you're over the Home link, but when you click on it, nothing happens.

213

When you press OK the link on the page will appear with the text being underlined. That's the normal behaviour with links. You're going to customise the links with CSS in Lesson 09.

19 Save the page and preview it in a web browser. Inspect the link by positioning your cursor over it. Your cursor should change to a hand icon which indicates a link on a page.

20 Back in Dreamweaver highlight the word **Eco News** in the horizontal menu section and navigate to the Insert panel for a change.

You're going to use another method for inserting links on a web page. This time using the Insert panel. As you remember from the previous introduction to the panels, there is a number of categories in the Insert panel and you're using Common for most tasks in the lessons as it provides you with most of the options for inserting all kinds of content. Look at the screenshots on the next page indicating different categories within Insert panel and the Common category that you're going to use:

214

21 With the **Eco News** text highlighted, choose **Hyperlink** from the list in the Insert panel (Common category).

NOTE: Be careful when you highlight the text, because anything you highlight will become a link (you don't want empty spaces to be links, too), so make sure you only highlight the words on their own, excluding the spaces between the words.

22 In the dialogue box that appears leave the Text as Eco News and in the **Link** section below click on the folder icon next to it. In the **Select File** dialogue box that appears select **news.html** and press **OK**. For **Target** click on the drop-down menu next to it and choose **_self**. Click OK.

23 Save the page and preview it in a web browser. Inspect the link by positioning your cursor over it. Your cursor should change to a hand icon which indicates a link on a page.

24 Click on the link and your web browser should open a new page - news.html in the same browser window (the page will just reload).

215

Now, you're going to add another link to the last menu element using yet another technique. This time, you're going to use the Properties panel.

25 Back in Dreamweaver highlight the word **Eco Tips** in the horizontal menu section and navigate to the Properties panel for a change. Find the section that reads **Link**.

26 Click on the folder icon next to it and select **tips.html** when the **Select File** dialogue box appears. Press OK. For **Target** click on the drop-down menu next to it and choose **_self**.

Congratulations! You have successfully added links to the horizontal menu and you should be able to navigate to other pages from the home page.

27 Now repeat steps you just learned to add links to horizontal menu on news.html and tips.html using one of the methods (choose one you prefer). Remember, you need to add menu on these pages first.

NOTE: On news.html, add "dummy" link to Eco News, on tips.html, add "dummy" link to Eco Tips. Home menu element should have a link on these two pages.

You may have noticed that the menu you create in other pages appears on the left instead of being on the right unless you recreate the CSS rule for it. You're going to do it the better way in the future lesson on Mastering CSS using an external stylesheet so you wouldn't have to do it for each page.

Create links to external websites

Both kinds of links, internal and external, work in a very similar way - they are defined in HTML code by the <a> tag. External links take the visitor to another website on the Internet or to a file (to be downloaded) from another website. And that's what you're going to do in this part of the lesson. You're going to create a link to an external website on the Internet. It's as simple as creating internal links. You can use any of the previously used methods. For example, you could use the Properties panel, this should be easy. So...

28   First open your web browser and navigate to the Google Maps. You're going to create a link to a map of the location of the company. This could be any address you wanted, as I am based in the UK I am going to use the address in England.

29   In my case, because I'm based in England, I chose **http://maps. google.co.uk** for the address but feel free to use the address that works best for your country.

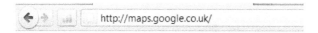

30 When Google Maps opens, type the address you're looking for (you can just type in a post code - I used the following post code SE14 5UB).

31 When the address loads on a page, in the top right corner of the page you will notice the chain icon as shown below.

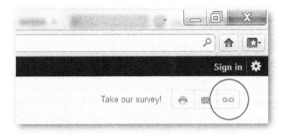

32 Click on the chain icon and copy the address to the clipboard as indicated on the screenshot below.

33 Navigate back to Dreamweaver and open **index.html** if it's not already opened. Place your cursor in the sidebar after the Join Now! button and press Enter to move the cursor into a new line and create a new paragraph of text.

34 Type **Find Us** and press Shift+Enter to move to the new line without creating a new paragraph and then type on **Google Maps**. This text will become a link that will point users to your location on a map.

35 Highlight the words Find Us on Google Maps and add a link to a map by navigating to the Properties panel and pasting the link (you can use Ctrl+V / Cmd+V). For **Target** click on the drop-down menu next to it and choose **_blank** this time. This will open the link in a new browser tab or a new browser window.

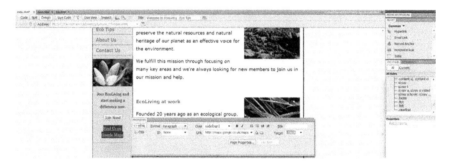

36 Save the page and preview it in a web browser. Inspect the link by positioning your cursor over it. Your cursor should change to a hand icon which indicates a link on a page.

37 Click on the link and your web browser should open a new page in a new tab (or window) with a map. Close the web browser and navigate back to Dreamweaver.

Congratulations! You have successfully added an external link that opens a map with your location. Well done.

In the future lesson you're going to use the new Widget Browser to insert a live map on your web page.

Now, you're going to create a link on an image.

38 Open **news.html** if it's not already open. Navigate to the sidebar and place your cursor at the beginning of the line that reads **Join EcoLiving...**

39 Press Enter and type on a new line above **Find out more about Energy Star Program by clicking on the logo above**.

40 Select the image and in the Properties panel type the link **http://www.energystar.gov**. For **Target** click on the drop-down menu next to it and choose **_blank**. This will open the link in a new browser tab or a new browser window.

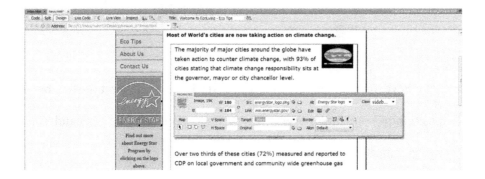

41 Save the page and preview it in a web browser. Click on the link and your web browser should open a new page in a new tab (or window). Close the web browser and navigate back to Dreamweaver.

Set up Email links

Adding Email links to your website allows your visitors to communicate with you in an easy way. Modern web browsers will even give the users a choice on how they want the email to be sent - either using their email client or using one of the web based email services. And, adding email links in Dreamweaver is very simple.

As usual, there are a number of ways to create Email links, it's very similar to creating hyperlinks. So, let's get started.

42 Open **index.html** if it's not already open. Navigate to the bottom of the page and place your cursor at the end of the section EcoLiving at work. Press Enter to create a new paragraph of text.

43 In the paragraph type **If you wish to join us, send us an email and we will get in touch with you**.

44 Highlight the text that reads **send us an email**. This will become an email link.

45 Navigate to the Insert panel and make sure the category (drop-down menu) is set to Common. Click on **Email Link**.

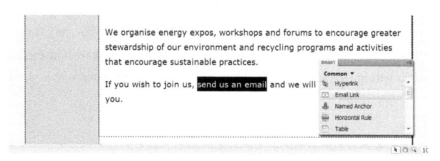

46 In the dialogue box that appears leave the Text as it is (it is the text that is highlighted on the page) and in the Email section type **contact@ ecoliving.org**. Press OK.

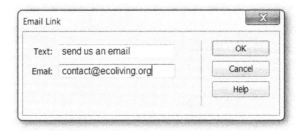

47 Save the page and preview it in a web browser. Check if the email link is working. Close the web browser and navigate back to Dreamweaver.

Congratulations! You have successfully inserted an Email link on a page. Now you're going to create a drop-down menu on one of the pages.

Insert drop-down menu

Imagine that you want to create an interactive drop-down menu on your website, that reveals submenu when the visitor clicks on one of the menu elements. To create this kind of menu, you would need HTML, CSS, and some JavaScript. If you were to create it from scratch, it would require a lot of knowledge of these technologies and the task would be very time consuming. Now, imagine creating it easily and effortlessly with just a few clicks within Dreamweaver. Wouldn't it be great? Now, it is possible within

Adobe Dreamweaver as the Spry Menu Bar is a part of Dreamweaver. Spry Menu Bar creates horizontal or vertical menu, using JavaScript and CSS, and it can be very easily added to your website in just a few steps. Because the Spry Menu Bar is based on JavaScript, it runs on all kinds of devices including mobile phones and tablets. And it runs on every computer of course.

What is Spry?

Spry is a JavaScript library for AJAX developed by Adobe. The Spry Framework offers easy to add and customise interface elements that can incorporate XML or HTML files. Now, you may be asking: What is AJAX. Let me explain.

AJAX (Asynchronous JavaScript and XML) is a combination of few technologies: JavaScript, XML, and DHTML. AJAX is used to develop Rich Internet Applications (RIAs), which create interactive content that can exchange data and update the page without reloading it. An example of AJAX technology that you definitely know is Google Mail, where you can update messages without reloading the page.

To find out more about Spry, go to Spry Framework for AJAX website: *http://labs.adobe.com/technologies/spry/*

To create drop-down menu with the Spry Menu Bar, you will replace the existing menu in the sidebar, and in the future lesson you will add it to other pages using Library Items.

48   If necessary, open **index.html**. Place your cursor in the menu in the sidebar.

223

49 Switch to Split View and highlight the entire menu in the code as shown on the screenshot below.

50 Press Delete key on your keyboard to remove it.

51 Keep the cursor blinking in the code after the opening tag for sidebar. Navigate to the Insert panel and change the category to Spry. Scroll down the menu until you find Spry Menu Bar.

52 Click on Spry Menu Bar and you should see a dialogue box where you need to select the layout you want to use. Select Vertical and press OK.

53 Switch back to Design View by clicking on the Design button in the top left corner of the document window.

You will see vertical drop-down menu in sidebar with grey background and four menu elements. You're going to customise it and you'll see how easy it is. Changing menu items can be easily achieved using Properties panel. If you look in the Properties panel, notice it displays properties for the Spry Menu (unless you deselect menu by clicking away from it, then you'll need to select it by clicking on cyan tab Spry Menu Bar: MenuBar1).

54 Start customising the menu elements using the Properties panel by highlighting the items and changing their names in Text area on the right as indicated on the screenshot below.

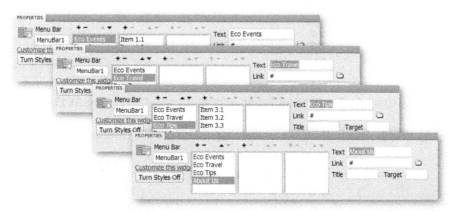

55 Now add one more menu item by clicking on the plus sign (+) above the first column in the Properties panel and type **Contact Us**.

56 Your Spry Menu should like this:

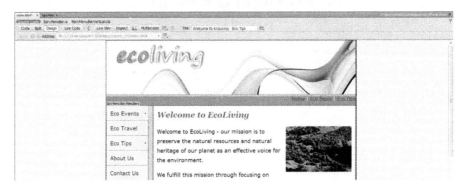

57 Now start customising the submenus. Navigate to the Properties panel with the Spry Menu selected and highlight Eco Events. You should see three submenu elements called Item 1.1, Item 1.2, and Item 1.3.

58 Highlight them one by one and change them to **Talks**, **Seminars**, and **Workshops**.

59 Highlight Eco Tips and change Item 3.1 and Item 3.2 to **At Home**, and **At Work**. Delete Item 3.3 by selecting it and clicking minus sign above (-).

60 Item 3.1 has another submenu so just delete Items 3.1.1 and 3.1.2.

226

61 Now you should have a drop-down menu with two items with submenus (Eco Events and Eco Tips).

62 Choose File > Save to save your page. Dreamweaver will display Copy Dependent Files dialogue box to let you know that the supporting files will be copied to your site folder. Just click OK.

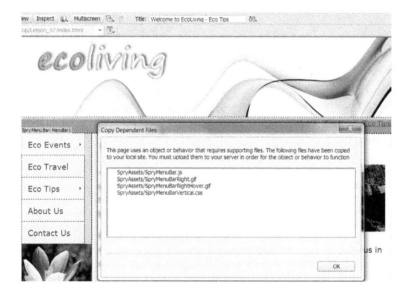

63 Click the Live View button on the top of the document window to test the drop-down menu you have created.

64 Mouse over the menu items to see the rollover effect and the submenus. Click the Live View button again to exit the Live View.

Notice that the menu items are not as wide as the sidebar and they have grey background. You're going to fix that in the next exercise.

Customising the Spry Menu Bar with CSS

Now that you've added and customised the menu items in the drop-down menu, it is time to style it. Every Spry element in Dreamweaver includes its own stylesheet that you use to modify the look of the element. Because the stylesheet is being attached to the page, you can modify it using the CSS Styles panel.

65 Navigate to the CSS Styles panel and find SpryMenuBarVertical.css (make sure you have All tab selected on the top of the CSS Styles panel).

66 Click on the plus sign (Windows) or arrow (Mac) to expand the Spry stylesheet (you can also click on the same icons to collapse your main stylesheet).

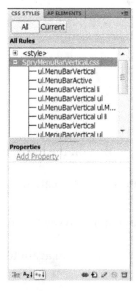

There are manu rules here, you will edit just a few of them. First thing you're going to change is the width of the menu.

67 Locate the rule **ul.MenuBarVertical** and change the width

property to **180px** as shown below.

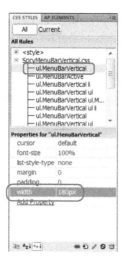

You may not notice any difference as this rule changes the size of the
menu container indicated by cyan border around the menu. Now, you're
going to change the width of the menu items.

68 Locate the rule **ul.MenuBarVertical li** and change the width

property to **180px**.

Now the width of the menu items changes. This is actually a bit too wide
as you won't see the green line on the edge between the sidebar and the
content column, so you'll make it 2 pixels narrower in the next step.

69 Locate the rule **ul.MenuBarVertical li** and change the width

property to **178px**. Now it looks better.

In the next step, you're going to change the menu background colour.

70 Locate the rule **ul.MenuBarVertical a** and click on the colour swatch next to the background-color property. When the colour picker appears click on the horizontal menu under the header to sample the background colour.

Now the drop-down menu should have green background colour that matches the background colour of the horizontal menu.

71 Within the same rule change the text colour by clicking on the colour swatch next to color property and select bright yellow.

72 Press the Live View button on the top of the document window to preview the page in the Live View. Notice that the background colour on rollover changes to blue.

73 Locate the rule **ul.MenuBarVertical a:hover, ul.MenuBarVertical a:focus** and click on the colour swatch next to the background-color property. When the colour picker appears choose bright yellow. Next click on the colour swatch next to color property and change it to green (you can click on the menu to sample the colur).

230

74 Repeat the last step for the next rule (very long rule that starts with **ul.MenuBarVertical a:MenuBarItemHover...**).

75 Press the Live View button on the top of the document window to preview the page in the Live View. Notice that the background colour on rollover changes to yellow.

Well done! You have just customised the drop-down menu in a few easy steps.

76 Finally run the page in a web browser to test it. When the dialogue box appears asking if you want to save changes, click Yes.

77 If you're using Internet Explorer you may see a yellow bar at the top of the browser window that says **To help protect your security, Internet Explorer has restricted this web page from running scripts....** IE will automatically block all scripting content, in this case JavaScript that's used to create drop-down menu, so to see it running you need to enable JavaScript by click on this yellow bar and choosing **Allow blocked content....**

78 That's the final result that you should see in your web browser.

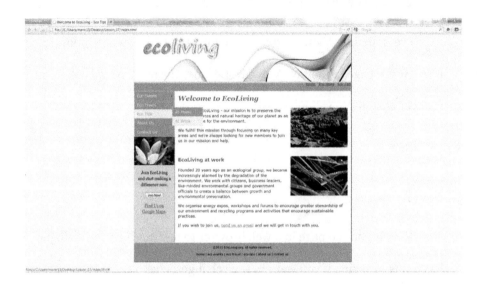

Review Questions

1. What does the target attribute in a link define?

2. What happens when someone clicks on an email link on a page?

3. What are different ways of inserting a link?

4. How do you create a link that doesn't link to anywhere but it allows you to check the link interaction?

Review Answers

1. **target** attribute defines whether the link is going to open in a new tab/window or is going to reload the content within the same window.

2. Modern web browsers will give the users a choice on how they want the email to be sent - either using their email client or using one of the web based email services.

3. You can insert a link from the Insert menu, Insert panel, and Properties panel.

4. Hash (#) symbol creates a so-called "dummy link" - a link that doesn't link to anywhere but allows you to check the link interaction, so you can see your cursor changing to a hand icon when you're over the link, but when you click on it, nothing happens.

Lesson 8

Mastering CSS

In this lesson you're going to master CSS and learn how to:

- differentiate internal vs external CSS

- move CSS rules to external stylesheet

- create new external stylesheet

- customise links with Pseudo-classes

- use the CSS Box Model

This lesson will take about 1 hour 30 minutes to complete.

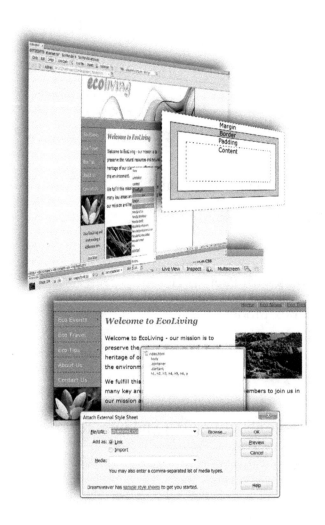

CSS Refresher

You already have some basics of Cascading Style Sheets (CSS) as you used some CSS in the other lesson and in the lessons that followed. As you have noticed, you will be using CSS all the time when designing websites. Every time you want to change the look of anything on the page, you will use CSS.

I would highly recommend using CSS Styles panel for all your CSS work - editing CSS rules as well as creating new ones and even creating stylesheets.

In this lesson, you're going to build on what you have already learned. You are also going to create an external stylesheet. So far you have been working with an internal stylesheet.

Internal vs External stylesheet

When you work with an internal stylesheet, the rules are created directly within a document and they are contained within the *<style>* tag. External stylesheet is a seperate document with all the rules and it has *.css* file extension.

One of the main differences between internal and external stylesheets is that the internal stylesheet only applies to one HTML document. If you had a website with six pages, you'd have six seperate stylesheets within all the pages. If you wanted to make some changes to the website, you'd need to make changes to every stylesheet seperately and you'd need to open every single page in Dreamweaver to make changes. With external stylesheet you'd have one stylesheet (one .css file) that would link to all the pages within the website and changing the stylesheet would update all the pages automatically. An external stylesheet can be attached to any number of HTML pages.

1 Launch Adobe Dreamweaver CS5, if it is not already open.

2 If you see the Welcome Screen, click on Dreamweaver Site button to define a new Site. If you don't see the Welcome Screen (you may have disabled it through the Dreamweaver Properties), choose Site > New Site from the menu. The Site Setup dialogue box appears.

3 In the Site Name field, type **Lesson_08**.

4 In the Local Site Folder field, click on the folder icon to the right and navigate to the **Lesson_08** folder containing the files for this lesson.

5 Select **Lesson_08** folder, and click Open (Windows) or Choose (Mac). Then, click Select (Windows) or Choose (Mac) to choose this folder as your local root folder.

6 Click the arrow next to the **Advanced Settings** category on the left to reveal a list of tabs. Select **Local Info** category and next to **Default Images folder** field, click the folder icon. When the dialogue box opens, navigate to the images folder located inside Lesson_08 folder and click Select (Windows) or Choose (Mac).

7 In the Site Setup dialogue box click Save.

8 Choose File > Open, and select **index.html**.

9 When the page opens, look into the CSS Styles panel. At the top of the panel, in the **All Rules** section, you'll find a stylesheet with a heading **<style>**. This means that this page uses an internal stylesheet.

NOTE: If the page uses an external stylesheet, instead of the heading **<style>** you'd see the name of the stylesheet, i.e. **stylesheet.css**.

10 Resize the CSS Styles panel so that you can see all the rules within the stylesheet. Don't worry about the Spry stylesheet, just focus on your main internal stylesheet.

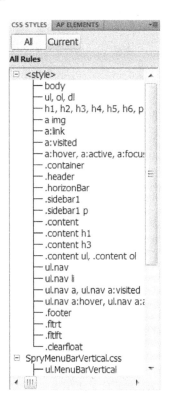

11 Let me share a great technique with you. You can use it to quickly find out if the page you have open uses an internal or external stylesheet. Place your cursor anywhere on the page. After a second or two, you should see the Code Navigator icon as shown below:

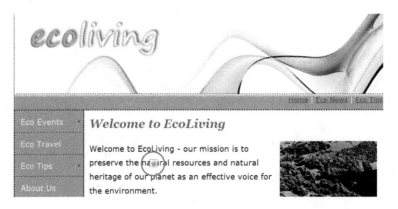

12 If you can see it, just click on it to display the Code Navigator. If you don't see it, you can use the keyboard shortcut - Ctrl+Alt+click on Windows or Cmd+Opt+click on Mac.

13 The Code Navigator window reads **index.html** and below you can see all rules that apply to the location of the cursor (you may see different rules).

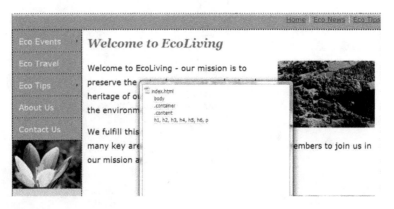

In the next step, you're going to move all the CSS rules to an external stylesheet (you're going to create one) and then you'll apply the newly created stylesheet to other pages within the website you're working on.

14 Navigate to the CSS Styles panel and highlight all the rules within <style> header by clicking on the first rule, then holding the Shift key down and clicking on the last rule (holding the Shift key down will highlight all the rules in between).

15 Now that all the rules are highlighted go to the menu in the top right corner of the panel and choose **Move CSS Rules…**.

16 In the Move to External Style Sheet dialogue box choose **A new style sheet** and click OK.

17 **Save Style Sheet File As** dialogue box will appear. In the File name field type **stylesheet** and click Save.

18 Nothing's changed on the page, but the page is now linked to an external stylesheet. Notice in the CSS Styles panel a new stylesheet called stylesheet.css.

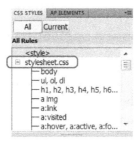

19 Now you need to tidy up a bit here. There are some remains of the old stylesheet as you can see from the <style> header at the top of the CSS Styles panel.

20 Highlight the <style> header and press Delete key on the keyboard to remove it.

Notice that the related documents toolbar at the top of the document window displays a new stylesheet and the HTML code changed as well:

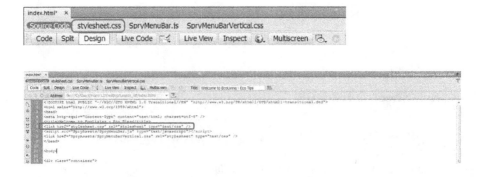

242

21 Now you're going to attach the newly created external stylesheet to other pages within the website.

22 Open **news.html**, highlight all the rules within <style> section in the CSS Styles panel and press Delete key to remove them. When prompted if you want to remove all the rules, click OK.

23 Now you can see what the page looks like without any styles.

24 In the CSS Styles panel click on the chain icon at the bottom to attach a stylesheet. When **Attach External Style Sheet** dialogue box appears click on Browse button and choose **stylesheet.css** as shown on the screenshots below:

25 Press OK to attach the stylesheet. The page should now look the same as before you removed the rules.

26 Repeat Steps 22 to 25 for **tips.html**.

27 Save pages and preview them in a web browser or using Live View.

Index.html is the only page that has drop-down menu, this will change in the next lesson on Templates, where you're going to explore Library Items. Now, you're going to create pseudo-classes to customise the links on the pages.

Customise links with Pseudo-classes

One of the great features of CSS is the ability to customise any page element. In case of Pseudo-classes, they're used to customise the behaviour of different states of the links on web pages. The Pseudo-classes define how the link should appear, depending on which state it is in.

There are four different states of links and they must be defined in certain order to be effective:

- a:link
- a:visited
- a:hover
- a:active

a:link	-	default display and behaviour of the hyperlink
a:visited	-	formatting after the link has been visited
a:hover	-	formatting while the cursor is over the link
a:active	-	formatting when the mouse clicked on link.

28 Because changing the behaviour of the links requires changing CSS and all the pages are now linked to the same stylesheet, it doesn't matter which HTML page you have open. Every HTML page points to the same stylesheet, so open one of the HTML pages and navigate to the CSS Styles panel.

244

29 In the CSS Styles panel find the first Pseudo-class **a:link**. Edit the rule by clicking on the pencil icon at the bottom of the CSS Styles panel or by double-clicking on the rule.

30 Change the colour of the link to yellow and notice that every link on the page changes (if you're on index.html the link to the map in the sidebar changes). That's because the rule applies to every link within a website. Change it back to original colour and press OK.

31 You're going to create a custom class for the links that appear in the horizontal menu near the top of the page. Start by selecting the **.horizonBar** rule in the CSS Styles panel.

32 Place your cursor within one of the links on the page and click on New CSS Rule icon at the bottom of the CSS Styles panel to create a new CSS rule.

33 In the New CSS Rule dialogue box set Selector Type to **Compound (based on your selection)**, Selector Name to **.horizonBar a:link**, and Rule Definition to **stylesheet.css**. Click Ok.

34 In the Type category set the colour to yellow, and Text-decoration to none. Click OK.

The rule you have just created applies only to the links within the horizontal menu (on every page).

35 Preview the pages in the web browser of your choice to see how they all update. When prompted to save any changes, accept.

When previewing the pages in a web browser, you may notice that some links are actually different colour. That's because we need to create another rule for visited links so they match the original links. That's what you're going to do in the next step.

36 Start by selecting the **.horizonBar a:link** rule in the CSS Styles panel. Place your cursor within one of the links on the page and click on New CSS Rule icon at the bottom of the CSS Styles panel to create a new CSS rule.

37 In the New CSS Rule dialogue box set Selector Type to **Compound (based on your selection)**, Selector Name to **.horizonBar a:visited**, and Rule Definition to **stylesheet.css**. Click OK.

38 In the Type category set the colour to yellow, and Text-decoration to none. Click OK.

39 Preview the pages in the web browser of your choice to see how they all update. When prompted to save any changes, accept.

246

You may have noticed that the menu appears a bit too high in the horizontal section. Now, you're going to move it down a bit with some more CSS. To do that, you're going to edit the horizontal menu rule.

40   Start by selecting the **.horizonBar** rule in the CSS Styles panel and then click on the Edit icon at the bottom of the CSS Styles panel.

41   Go to the Box category when the CSS Rule Definition dialogue box opens and deselect **Same for all** for Padding.

42   Type **5px** for Padding Top and change the Height to **35px**. Click Apply. Don't close the dialogue box yet.

43   The menu is now a bit lower and it looks nicely centred but it is too close to the right edge of the page. Give it some Padding on the right to move it away from the edge, i.e. **20px**, and change the Width to **930px**. Click OK.

CSS Box Model

Now you're going to learn about the CSS Box Model. It is the reason why when you changed the padding in the previous steps, you also needed to change the width or the height.

When designing web pages, consider all HTML elements as boxes on a page. Term "Box Model" is used when talking about the layout. The CSS Box Model is a box wrapping around each HTML element on a page.

It consists of four main elements:

- margin
- border
- padding
- content

as shown on the image below:

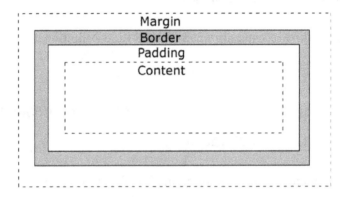

When you set the width or the height of the element, you just set the size of the content area. Let me give you an example. Here's an example code:

```
width: 200px;

padding: 10px;
```

You would have thought that the elements width would be 200px, but it's not if you test it in a web browser. Here's what happens and how the CSS Box Model works:

- 200px width + 10px padding on left + 10px padding on right = 220px

That's why when you added padding, you had to change the width or height of the element. The same applies if you have margin being applied.

248

Back to the website you're working on, test it in a web browser and if you're not happy with padding, change it. Remember to alter the width or height when changing the padding.

44 Create additional Compound rules for **.horizonBar a:hover**, and

.horizonBar a:active by repeating steps 36 to 38.

Use any colours you like, but use different colours for hover state and active state so that the link looks different when the user places the cursor over the link and when the user clicks on it.

45 Preview the pages in the web browser of your choice to see how they all update. When prompted to save any changes, accept.

Congratulations! You have succesfully customised the links on the pages using CSS. Now you're going to create your own custom CSS class to change the alignment of the images on the pages. You'll see how easy it is.

46 Navigate to the CSS Styles panel and find the rules **fltrt** and **fltlft**. Highlight them and delete them by clicking on the bin icon at the bottom of the CSS Styles panel.

47 The images should change their positions when you delete the CSS rules. That's fine. You're going to create your own custom classes.

48 Click on New CSS Rule icon in the CSS Styles panel.

49 Set the Selector Type to **Class**, Selector Name to **floatRight**, and Rule Definition to **stylesheet.css**.

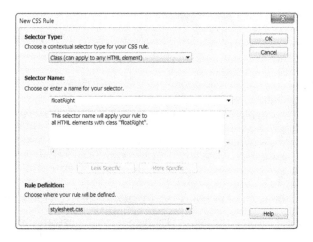

50 Go to the Box category and set the Float property to **right**. In the Margin property, set it to **10px margin** on left. Click OK.

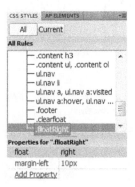

51 Open **index.html** if it isn't open already. Select the first image in the right column (forest.jpg), and apply the newly created class through the Properties panel as shown below.

52 Repeat Steps 48 to 50 to create another class **floatLeft**, this time setting the Float property to **left** and setting **10px margin** on right.

53 Apply newly created class to the second image on the page (grass. jpg), so it aligns to the left and the text is floating around it.

If your image appears next to the heading instead of being placed next to the paragraph as on the screenshot below, you'll need to move it. If the image is positioned next to the paragraph, you can skip the next step.

251

54 Click on the image on the page and simply drag it and drop it before the first line of the paragraph. When the cursor appears before the text **Founded**, release the mouse button to drop the image. Well done!

55 Open **news.html** if it isn't open already. Select the first image in the right column, and apply **floatRight** class through the Properties panel.

56 Repeat the process for other images on the page aligning them to the right and to the left.

57 Open **tips.html** if it isn't open already. Select the first image in the right column, and apply **floatRight** class through the Properties panel..

58 Select the second image in the right column and align it to the right as well using the same method as above.

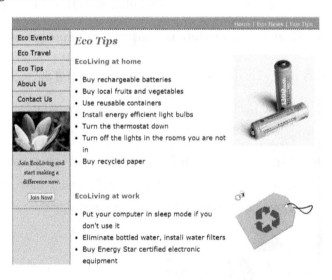

59 Now save all the changes within all the pages (if you still have all the pages open) by choosing **File > Save All**.

252

Now, you're going to make a few adjustments to the footer. You're going to change the text colour and add links to the text menu in the footer.

60 Open **index.html** if it isn't open already. Scroll the page down so that you can see the footer. Notice that the text is black and hard to read against the green background.

61 Navigate to the CSS Styles panel and find the footer rule. Edit it.

62 In the Type category change the text colour to bright yellow. Click OK to accept the changes.

63 Highlight the word **home** in the footer and add a link to it pointing to **index.html**. Set the target property to **_self**.

64 Repeat the process for **eco tips**.

65 Because the other pages don't exist, when adding link type hash symbol (#) in the link field, and set the target to **_self** as well.

NOTE: You're going to create additional pages in the next lesson on working with templates.

As you can see from the screenshot above, the links are now black with an underline. That's the default behaviour of the links on the page. You're going to change it now with some more custom CSS.

66 Create new custom Compound Rules for the links in the footer by following Steps 36 to 39, but this time using footer instead of horizMenu when creating new CSS rules.

67 When creating new Compound Rules for the links in the footer, change the text colour and remove the underline from the original link.

Here are examples of the rules that I have created:

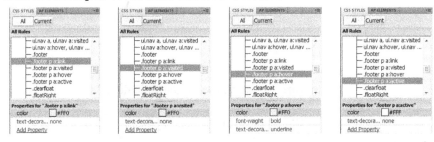

Because you have created these rules in the external stylesheet (stylesheet. css), you don't have to do it for all other pages as all the pages are using the same external stylesheet. Can you see the benefits of using external CSS?

The only thing is, the other pages don't have links attached to the text menu in the footer.

68 Open **news.html** and apply the links to the text menu in the footer as in Steps 63 to 65.

69 Repeat the same process for **tips.html**.

70 Now all the three pages you have created should have links attached to the text menu in the footer.

71 Preview the pages in the web browser of your choice to see how they all update. When prompted to save any changes, accept.

It's time to tidy up a bit. If you look through the pages, you will notice that some pages still have some remains of the old internal stylesheet - tips.html and news.html. You're going to remove these remains to keep just the external CSS.

72 Open **tips.html** and highlight **<style>** header in the CSS Styles panel. Press Delete key on the keyboard to remove it.

73 Repeat the same process for **news.html**.

74 Save the changes by choosing **File > Save All**.

Here's another thing. If you scroll down the pages, you'll notice that there is not much space at the bottom of the page, between the content and the footer. In the next step, you're going to increase the space by using CSS.

75 Navigate to the CSS Styles panel and find the **content** rule. It doesn't matter which page you have open, because all the pages use the same stylesheet.

76 Edit the **content** rule and give it **padding** on the bottom **30px**. Click OK to accept the changes.

77 Preview the pages in a web browser of your choice and notice how the spacing changed.

78 If you open **news.html**, you'll notice that there is a table near the bottom of the page and it sits next to the left age. Increase the spacing between the content and the border by adding **20px padding** on the left to the **content** rule.

As soon as you increase padding, you'll notice that the entire page shifts, the content column moves.

That's because as you add padding (or margin), you need to alter the width or the height of the element - CSS Box Model from earlier in this lesson. So what you need to do here is to alter the width of the content element and that's what you're going to do in the next step.

78 Finish this page by changing the width of the content element from 770px to **750px**. Save all the changes.

Congratulations! You have successfully completed another lesson. Well done.

Review Questions

1. Where are the CSS rules created when you work with an internal stylesheet?

2. What are the Pseudo-classes used for?

3. Where would you find the **Move CSS Rules...** option?

4. How can you quickly bring up the Code Navigator?

Review Answers

1. When you work with an internal stylesheet, the rules are created directly within a document and they are contained within the *<style>* tag.

2. Pseudo-classes are used to customise the behaviour of different states of the links on web pages. The Pseudo-classes define how the link should appear, depending on which state it is in.

3. You can find the **Move CSS Rules....** option in the menu in the top right corner of the CSS Styles panel.

4. To quickly bring up the Code Navigator, you can use the keyboard shortcut - Ctrl+Alt+click on Windows or Cmd+Opt+click on Mac

Lesson 9

Templates

In this lesson you're going to learn how to be more productive and how to:

- create Dreamweaver templates

- create editable regions in templates

- create new pages from a template

- update templates

- insert and customise the table

This lesson will take about 1 hour to complete.

Dreamweaver templates

What are templates you may ask? Templates are like master pages that are used to produce child pages. Templates are great for quickly creating web pages within a site. Template has editable and non-editable regions within a page. The usual workflow for designing web pages is to start by creating the first page and then converting it into a template. Then, you create all pages from a template.

You could create a template starting with a blank page, but it is much better to take an existing page and convert it into a template.

1 Launch Adobe Dreamweaver CS5, if it is not already open.

2 If you see the Welcome Screen, click on Dreamweaver Site button to define a new Site. If you don't see the Welcome Screen (you may have disabled it through the Dreamweaver Properties), choose Site > New Site from the menu. The Site Setup dialogue box appears.

3 In the Site Name field, type **Lesson_09**.

4 In the Local Site Folder field, click on the folder icon to the right and navigate to the **Lesson_09** folder containing the files for this lesson.

5 Select **Lesson_09** folder, and click Open (Windows) or Choose (Mac). Then, click Select (Windows) or Choose (Mac) to choose this folder as your local root folder.

6 Click the arrow next to the **Advanced Settings** category on the left to reveal a list of tabs. Select **Local Info** category and next to **Default Images folder** field, click the folder icon. When the dialogue box opens, navigate to the images folder located inside Lesson_08 folder and click Select (Windows) or Choose (Mac).

7 In the Site Setup dialogue box click Save.

8 Choose File > Open, and select **news.html**.

The first step now is going to be converting an existing page into a template and then defining editable regions within a page.

9 When the page opens, choose **File > Save as Template....**

10 Save As Template dialogue box will appear. Make sure the name of your site - Lesson_09 - appears in the **Site** drop-down menu. In the **Save as** field type ecoLiving_template. In the **Description** field type **Main Template for EcoLiving website with 2 columns sidebar on left**. Click Save.

11 A dialogue box asking whether you want to update links appears. Click Yes to update links.

Templates are stored in a seperate folder within your site. When you create a template, Dreamweaver creates a new folder called Templates and inserts the newly created template into this folder. That's why you see the dialogue box asking whether you want to update links.

12 The page still looks the same, nothing changed within the actual

page, but the name of the file has changed - the page is now **ecoLiving_**

template.dwt. Notice the file extension - **.dwt** - for Dreamweaver

templates.

Template creates a dynamic link to the pages that you're going to create.
When the template changes, Dreamweaver is going to update all the
pages that were created from a template dynamically. This is one of the
amazing features of Dreamweaver templates, a great time saver. Now
what you need to do is to create editable regions within the template.

Create editable regions

When you converted a page into a template, Dreamweaver started
treating all the content on the page as part of the master design. What
this basically means is that if you were to create new pages from a
template, they would all have the same content that would be locked and
you wouldn't be able to edit it. This is great for some parts of the page. If
you look at the design you'll notice that elements like header and footer
are not going to change between the pages, so if these elements are locked
on the new pages, then it's fine. But what about the rest of the content?
You don't want to have the same content in the right column on every
single page, do you? That's where you'll create editable regions to define
which areas of the template are going to be editable and are going to
change from page to page.

Before you start inserting editable regions plan it and decide how many you're going to create and where will they be created. In this case, you're going to create two editable regions: one in the sidebar *(div.sidebar1)* and one in the content area *(div.content)*.

13 Start by placing your cursor in the sidebar and then using the tag inspector click on **<div.sidebar1>**.

14 Before you create editable region in the sidebar you need to double check that the entire sidebar is selected. Navigate to the Code view and check if the entire sidebar code is highlighted.

15 If the entire sidebar code is highlighted, as on the screenshot above, then choose **Insert > Template Objects > Editable Region**.

16 When **New Editable Region** dialogue box appears, type **sidebar** and press OK.

264

17 Navigate back to the Design view and notice the cyan tab with the name appear in the sidebar. That's the indication of the editable region.

18 Before you create the second editable region, you will remove some content from the page as there is too much content here that you don't need in a template. Remove everything except the first section so the page looks like on a screenshot below.

19 Place your cursor in the right column and then using the tag inspector click on **\<div.content\>**.

Once again before you create editable region in the right column you need to double check that the entire column is selected.

20 Navigate to the Code view and check if the entire column code is highlighted as indicated on the screenshot below.

21 If the entire right column code is highlighted, as on the screenshot above, then choose **Insert > Template Objects > Editable Region**.

22 When **New Editable Region** dialogue box appears, type **mainContent** and press OK.

23 Navigate back to the Design view and notice the cyan tab with the name appear in the right column. That's your second editable region.

You have successfully created two editable regions within the template. Now it's time ti save it and start creating pages from the template.

24 Save the template by choosing **File > Save**. Close it to get back to the Welcome screen.

Create new pages from Template

Let me explain something before you start creating new pages from the template you have just created. Before you start creating new pages, you need to understand that the process of creating new pages is very important. Here's why:

In the years that I have been training Dreamweaver and designing websites I have met so many people who make the same mistake and I want to warn you here so that you don't do the same. Here's what many people do:

They create a template, and then they start editing it by adding new content and then they save it as a new page. This is a big mistake because this breaks the link between the template and the new page that's being created. Once you've created a template and defined editable regions, save it and close it. Do not open it unless you want to make some changes to the locked regions. The right way of creating pages from a template is to use New document dialogue box. That's what you're going to do now.

25 Choose **File > New** or press Ctrl+N on Windows, Cmd+N on Mac.

26 When the **New Document** dialogue box appears, select **Page from Template** in the left column. You should see the preview of the template on the right hand side with the description below it. Click **Create**.

That's the process you'll be going through with all the pages. You'll be creating all new pages from a template by using New Document dialogue box. Now it's time to start adding content to the newly created page.

27 Once you pressed Create, Dreamweaver opens a new page that's ready to start editing. Notice the name of the template in the top right corner of the page. You're going to create Eco News page.

28 The page you're working on should have some content from Eco News page already in place, so what you need to do is add more content. Start by placing your cursor at the end of the content in the right column.

29 In the File panel, double-click on ecoNews.txt in the Text folder to open the file. The file will open in Dreamweaver.

Because the first section is already on the page, highlight all the rest and copy it to the clipboard by choosing **Edit > Copy** or pressing **Ctrl+C** on Windows or **Cmd+C** on Mac.

30 Back to the new page, paste the text by choosing **Edit > Paste** or **Ctrl+V** on Win / **Cmd+V** on Mac.

31 Save the page as **news.html**. Because the news page already exists, Dreamweaver will prompt you if you want to overwrite the file. Click **Yes**.

32 In the Title field, select the text Eco Tips and change it to **Eco News**.

33 Highlight the line that starts with **Dutch study shows...** and format it as **Heading 2**.

34 Highlight the line that starts with **UN study shows** and format it as **Heading 2** as well.

268

35 Save the page and preview it in the web browser of your choice. When prompted to save any changes, accept.

36 Just before you close this file, make one more change. Change all headings to **Heading 3** instead of Heading 2. They should get smaller and turn green colour that matches the colour scheme of the website.

37 Save and close the page. That's what the page should look like.

Now you're going to create another page - Eco Tips.

38 Choose **File > New** or press Ctrl+N on Windows, Cmd+N on Mac.

39 When the **New Document** dialogue box appears, select **Page from Template** in the left column. Click **Create**.

40 In the Files panel, double-click on ecoTips.txt in the Text folder to open the file. The file will open in Dreamweaver.

269

41 Highlight all the text and copy it to the clipboard by choosing **Edit >
Copy** or pressing **Ctrl+C** on Windows or **Cmd+C** on Mac.

42 Back to the new page, highlight all the content in the right column and
delete it.

43 Paste the text by choosing **Edit > Paste** or **Ctrl+V** on Win / **Cmd+V**
on Mac.

44 Save the page as **tips.html**. Because the tips page already exists,
Dreamweaver will prompt you if you want to overwrite the file. Click **Yes**.

45 Highlight the line that reads **Eco Living at home** and format it as
Heading 3.

46 Highlight the line that reads **Eco Living at work** and format it as
Heading 3 as well.

47 In the Title field, this time you don't need to do anything as this is Eco
Tips page.

48 Finally, Highlight the line that reads **Eco Tips** and format it as
Heading 1.

49 Now quickly turn the text within these two sections to unordered lists.
Highlight all the text under Eco Living at home and turn it into an unordered
list.

50 Highlight all the text under Eco Living at work and turn it into an unordered list as well.

51 The page should now look like on the screenshot below.

52 Save the page and preview it in Live View. When done, close the page to return to the Welcome screen.

Have you noticed that when you preview a page in a web browser, there is no indication that the page was created from a template? The tabs for editable regions or the name of the template in the top right corner of the page only appear in Dreamweaver, these are Dreamweaver features. You won't see them in a web browser.

Now you're going to introduce some changes to the template and you'll see how Dreamweaver will update all the pages for you as you change the template. A fantastic time saver!

53 Open the template by clicking on its name in the Welcome screen or by double-clicking on the template in the Templates folder in the Files panel.

54 As you move your cursor around, notice that you can click anywhere and change anything you want. Now, try to do the same with one of the pages. Close the template.

55 Open one of the pages you have created - news.html or tips.html.

56 Move your cursor around and notice that header and footer areas are locked and you cannot click in there. That's the beauty of using templates.

57 Open the template once again, scroll down the page and place your cursor in the footer. You're going to make a change in the footer.

58 Place your cursor at the beginning, before the copyright symbol and type **Copyrighted**.

59 Close the template and when prompted to save the changes, click **Yes**.

60 You should now see the **Update Template Files** dialogue box. Two pages you have just created should appear within the dialogue box. When you click Update, Dreamweaver will update both pages. Click **Update**.

61 Once you click Upate, you'll see a dialogue box - Update Pages.

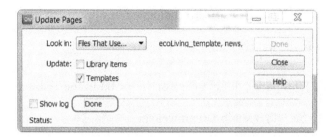

62 In just a second or two, you'll see the message saying Done in the bottom part of the dialogue box as encircled on the screenshot above.

63 If it says Done, it means the pages have been updated. You can see the names of the pages that were updated at the top of the dialogue box. Click Close.

64 Open one of the pages and preview it. Notice how the footer updated.

Every time you change the template, it will update all the pages that were created from a template. Notice that the index.html hasn't changed. That's because this page hasn't been created from a template.

In the next section of this lesson you're going to create another page from a template - index.html.

65 Choose **File > New** or press Ctrl+N on Windows, Cmd+N on Mac.

66 When the **New Document** dialogue box appears, select **Page from Template** in the left column. Click **Create**.

67 In the Files panel, double-click on index.txt in the Text folder to open the file. The file will open in Dreamweaver.

68 Highlight all the text and copy it to the clipboard by choosing **Edit > Copy** or pressing **Ctrl+C** on Windows or **Cmd+C** on Mac.

69 Back to the new page, highlight all the content in the right column and delete it.

70 Paste the text by choosing **Edit > Paste** or **Ctrl+V** on Win / **Cmd+V** on Mac.

71 Save the page as **index.html**. Because the index page already exists, Dreamweaver will prompt you if you want to overwrite the file. Click **Yes**.

72 Highlight the line that reads **Welcome to EcoLiving** and format it as **Heading 1**.

73 Highlight the line that reads **Eco Living at work** and format it as **Heading 3**.

74 Place the cursor at the beginning of the first line of the paragraph and insert an image - **climateChange.gif**. As Alternative text type **Climate change**. Press OK.

274

75 Align the newly inserted image to the right by applying a **floatRight** class to it.

76 Save the page and test it in a web browser. Navigate between the pages.

NOTE: If the link to one of the pages doesn't work, open the template and assign a link to a menu element.
By now, you should be able to navigate between the home page, news page, and tips page.

77 Create one more page from a template. You're going to create Eco Events page.

78 Follow the steps for creating a new page from a template - steps 65, 66, and 69.

79 Once you've deleted the content on the page, type the heading **Eco Events** and turn it into **Heading 1**.

80 Move the cursor to a new line and insert a table under the heading by choosing **Insert > Table** (alternatively you can use a keyboard shortcut **Ctrl+Alt+T on Win** or **Cmd+Alt+T** on Mac).

81 When Table dialogue box appear, use the settings as shown on the screenshot on the next page.

82 In the top row type in each column: **Date**, **Event**, **Location**, **Price**.

83 In the second row type: **January 1**, **New Year's Parade**, **Trafalgar Square**, **Free**.

84 Fill the additional rows with data as shown on the screenshot below.

To add additional rows, just press Tab key on your keyboard in the last cell.

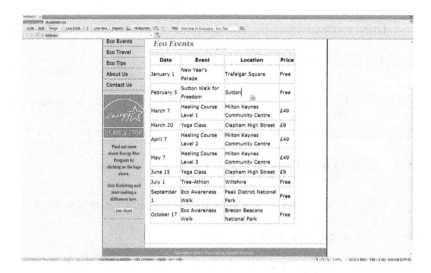

85 Save and test the page. Save it as **events.html**.

Now, you're going to customise the table a bit.

86 Place your cursor inside the table and select **<table>** tag in the tag inspector. Change the table's width to **650px** using the Properties panel.

87 To match the look of the website, give the table green border. With the table highlighted, give it an ID **events** in the top right corner of the Properties panel as shown below.

88 Create a new CSS rule - a Compound rule **.content #events** and add a green border around the table giving it **1px** on top and left, **3px** on bottom and right.

89 Remove the default table border by placing the cursor inside the table, selecting the **<table>** tag in the tag inspector and typing **0** for border in the Properties panel.

90 You're going to finish this lesson with one more technique in CSS. You're going to add border to all the cells inside the table.

91 Create New CSS Rule in the CSS Styles panel, set it as **Compound** and call it **.content #events td**.

92 Give it a border of **1px solid #060** and set the Height to **50px**. Click OK.

93 Save the page and preview it. The table should now have a nice green border inside.

Congratulations! You have successfully completed another lesson. Well done.

Review Questions

1. Where are the templates stored?

2. How do you insert editable regions?

3. Why would you create editable regions within a template?

4. What will happen when you change the template?

Review Answers

1. Templates are stored in a seperate folder within your site. When you create a template, Dreamweaver creates a new folder called Templates and inserts the newly created template into this folder.

2. Insert > Template Objects > Editable Region.

3. You create editable regions to define which areas of the template are going to be editable and are going to change from page to page.

4. Every time you change the template, it will update all the pages that were created from a template.

Lesson 10

Sound and Video

In this lesson you're going to learn how to incorporate media into your website and how to:

- add sounds
- add Flash animations
- add videos

This lesson will take about 40 minutes to complete.

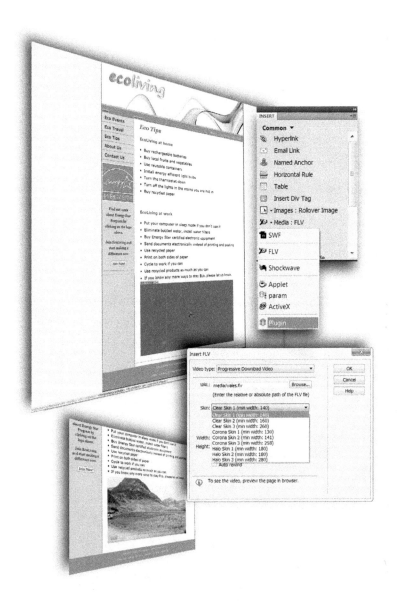

Media on web pages

Media are getting more and more common on most websites nowadays. Adding audio and video on your pages is quite easy and you're going to learn it in just a moment. Adobe has been trying to make adding media to web pages easier and easier, and every new version of Dreamweaver brings improvements in the way we insert media on pages.

Before starting inserting media on your pages, there are a few things you need to be aware of. First of all, media files can be very large, especially videos so you need to plan a bit and decide on how you're going to incorporate your videos on the pages. And you will need to decide what file formats to use for your sounds/videos. We're going to discuss it more later in the lesson.

1 Launch Adobe Dreamweaver CS5, if it is not already open.

2 On Welcome Screen, click on Dreamweaver Site button to define a new Site. If you don't see Welcome Screen, choose Site > New Site from the menu. The Site Setup dialogue box appears.

3 In the Site Name field, type **Lesson_10**.

4 In the Local Site Folder field, click on the folder icon to the right and navigate to the **Lesson_10** folder containing the files for this lesson.

5 Select **Lesson_10** folder, and click Open (Windows) or Choose (Mac). Then, click Select (Windows) or Choose (Mac) to choose this folder as your local root folder.

6 Click the arrow next to the **Advanced Settings** category on left to reveal tabs. Select **Local Info** category and next to **Default Images folder** field, click the folder icon. When dialogue box opens, navigate to the images folder located inside Lesson_10 folder and click Select (Windows) or Choose (Mac).

7 In the Site Setup dialogue box click Save.

8 Choose File > Open, and select **index.html**.

Adding sounds

The first step now is going to be incorporating a sound into a web page.

Some people don't like sounds on web pages, especially if the sounds keep on looping or play for a very long time. That's why, for this exercise, you're going to use a sound that is less than a minute long and it is not going to loop. Before you add a sound to your web pages, you should also be aware that your sound will serve a purpose and will add value to the page. Using a short, smooth sound, that doesn't annoy the visitors to your website, may sound like a good idea. Of course, sound makes a lot of sense for websites for musicians, games, and websites aimed at children.

In this lesson, you're going to add short, soothing intro sound on the home page. You're going to practise two methods of adding sounds to the page:
- inserting a sound with a controller
- inserting a sound that will play in the background

First, you will insert a sound with a controller so that the visitor will be able to play and pause the sound as well as to change the volume/mute it.

Second, you will insert a sound that will play automatically in the background and will require no interaction from the user. Even more than that, the user will not be able to control it, the sound will start playing automatically when the page loads.

You're going to start by inserting a sound with a controller in the sidebar.

9   With index.html page open, navigate to the sidebar and place your cursor at the beginning of the line that reads **Join EcoLiving**.

10   Press Enter on your keyboard to move the text to the next line and then move the cursor up to the empty line above and type **Listen to our Intro** as shown on the screenshot below.

11   Navigate to the Insert panel (Common category) and choose Media > Plugin as shown on the screenshot on the next page.

Now, you may be wondering why you need to choose Plugin and why there is no Sound option in the Insert panel under Media, am I correct? Is that what you're thinking now? I think you are. Dreamweaver doesn't have a specific option for inserting sound files. Adding sound to web pages is a bit confusing as it will require the user to have a plugin installed within their web browser. In this lesson, you are going to insert a **.wav** file, because it is a short sound and this file format is widely supported in web browsers. Another file format that is commonly used on web pages is mp3.

12 Select File dialogue box is going to open, so you can select the file that will play. Navigate to the media folder and choose **intro.wav**. Click **OK**.

13 Plugin icon will appear on the page and your Properties panel should read **Plugin, 1171K** in the top right corner.

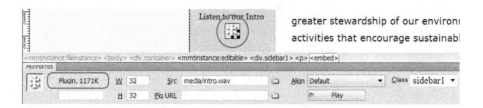

Because you are inserting this sound file in form of a music player, you will need to decide on the size of the player using the available space in the sidebar. You will be testing the page in a web browser as you make changes to the size of the player to make sure you're happy with the way it looks on the page, especially with the height of it.

14 Select the plugin object on the page if it's not still selected and change its size using the Properties panel. Try **150px** for Width (**W**) and leave the Height (**H**) at **32px** for now.

15 Preview the page in the web browser.

16 The Width looks good, but the player is too high and it displays grey area above and below the player. Adjust the Height to **16px** and it should look fine.

17 You may want to preview the page in different web browsers if possible, i.e. Firefox, Explorer, Safari, Opera, or Chrome to make sure the music player displays correctly.

Here's the screenshot from Firefox 4 and Explorer 8 on Windows.

What if you want to sound to play in the background? It plays automatically anyway, so you could easily embed it into the page. You're going to do it now in the next step.

18 Start by removing the plugin you have inserted. Highlight the plugin and the text above, and press Delete key to remove it.

The technique you're going to use here requires finding a good place for your sound on the page. It will appear on the page and you will make it very small, hardly seen, so it may be a good idea to place it inside the text.

19 Place your cursor inside the main text on the page as shown on the screenshot below.

20 Insert the sound by using the Plugin option in the Insert panel as in the steps 11-12.

288

21 Plugin icon will appear on the page. Select the plugin object on the page if it's not selected and change its size to **1px** by **1px** using the Properties panel.

22 Now you won't see it on the page, but it will still play. Well done!

23 Preview the page in the web browser to test it.

As you preview the page in the web browser, the sound will start playing automatically in the background. You have successfully added a sound to the web page. Time to add a video to the page.

Adding videos

Before you add videos to your web pages, you need to understand that videos can use a lot of your web space and bandwidth. Every time your video is being watched, it uses the bandwidth (or monthly traffic as it is also often called) that is allocated to your website through the hosting provider.

Check with your hosting provider how much bandwidth they offer you with your hosting package to avoid extra charges.

On the next page you'll see an example of a bandwidth provided by one of the hosting providers, the one I use:

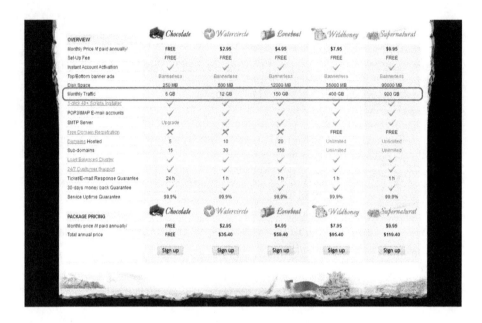

The video you're going to add to a web page is a video called wales.flv. It is a video in Flash video format as Flash is the most widely used file format for video distribution online. The Flash format requires an extra component to play. But this component comes preinstalled with web browsers like Firefox and Internet Explorer.

24 Close **index.html**. You don't need it anymore.

25 Open **tips.html**. You're going to add a video on this page.

26 Scroll to the bottom of the page and place your cursor under the last list.

27 Press Enter on your keyboard to move the cursor to the new line. If the new list element is being created, then press Enter once again to create a new paragraph of text.

28 With the cursor at the bottom of the page placed navigate to the

Insert panel and choose **Media > FLV**.

29 When the **Insert FLV** dialogue box appears, leave Video type set as

Progressive Download Video and next to **URL** click on **Browse**.

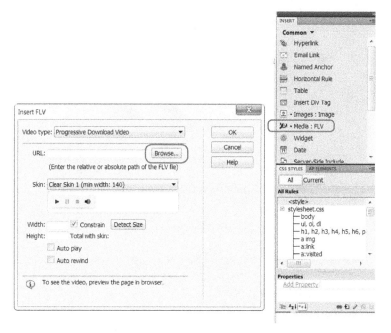

30 In the Select FLV dialogue box choose **wales.flv** from media folder.

31 Back to Insert FLV dialogue box, click the Detect Size button to

detect the dimensions of the video to choose the appropriate skin. It

should read **640px** Width and **360px** Height.

32 Now you can choose from three different skins and each skin comes

in three different sizes as shown on the screenshot on the next page.

33 Choose one of the skins and click OK to insert the video on the page.

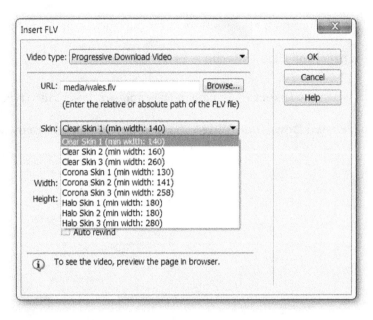

34 The video should fit nicely on the page in the right column.

35 Preview the page in the web browser to preview the video. You will see the dialogue box saying that some files that are required will be coppied to your local site. Just press OK.

36 Back to Dreamweaver, with the video on the page selected, look in the Properties panel. If you want the video to play automatically, just check **Auto Play**.

NOTE: Auto Play should remain unchecked, so the visitor to your website can decide if they want to play the video or not.
If you decide, you want to use a different skin, you can change it in the Properties panel at any time.

37 Save and preview the page once again.

292

That's what the page should look like back in Dreamweaver.

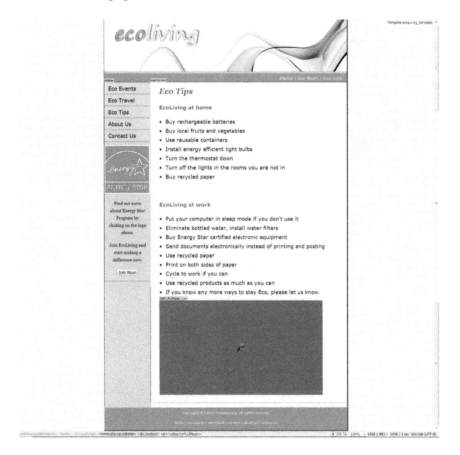

Review Questions

1. Where would you find an option to insert a sound on a page?

2. How do you change the size of the sound player?

3. Can you change the skin for the video player? If yes, then how?

Review Answers

1. Navigate to the Insert panel (Common category) and choose Media > Plugin.

2. Select the plugin object on the page and change its size using the Properties panel.

3. If you decide, you want to use a different skin, you can change it in the Properties panel.

Lesson 11

Spry

In this lesson you're going to learn how to implement Spry into your website and how to:

- add Spry menu bar

- add Spry Accordion

- add Spry tabbed panels

- add Spry Effects

This lesson will take about 1 hour 30 minutes to complete.

What is Spry?

The Spry (Spry Framework) is an open source Ajax framework developed by Adobe, and it is used in creating Rich Internet Applications. What differs Spry from other JavaScript frameworks is that it has been developed with web designers, not web developers in mind. Adobe developed Spry because other Ajax frameworks were quite complex and hard to understand.

Because Spry was designed with web designers in mind, anyone with a bit of experience with Dreamweaver can create Rich Internet Applications. Spry uses what you already know: HTML and CSS, maybe a bit of JavaScript as well. Spry is a set of JavaScript libraries, that need to be included when testing and exporting to the web server.

There are three main Spry categories:
- Spry Effects, i.e. Slide, Fade
- Spry Widgets, i.e. Accordion, Tabbed panels
- Spry Data, using data to populate the page, i.e. XML

The good news is, when adding Spry elements to your pages, no plug-ins are required.

1 Launch Adobe Dreamweaver CS5, if it is not already open.

2 If you see the Welcome Screen, click on Dreamweaver Site button to define a new Site. If you don't see the Welcome Screen (you may have disabled it through the Dreamweaver Properties), choose Site > New Site from the menu. The Site Setup dialogue box appears.

3 In the Site Name field, type **Lesson_11**.

4 In the Local Site Folder field, click on the folder icon to the right and navigate to the **Lesson_11** folder containing the files for this lesson.

5 Select **Lesson_11** folder, and click Open (Windows) or Choose (Mac). Then, click Select (Windows) or Choose (Mac) to choose this folder as your local root folder.

6 Click the arrow next to the **Advanced Settings** category on the left to reveal a list of tabs. Select **Local Info** category and next to **Default Images folder** field, click the folder icon. When the dialogue box opens, navigate to the images folder located inside Lesson_11 folder and click Select (Windows) or Choose (Mac).

7 In the Site Setup dialogue box click Save.

8 Choose File > Open, and select **index.html**.

Spry menu bar

In Lesson 7 you have inserted the Spry menu bar, so you are already familiar with the process of adding drop-down menu to the web page. This time, you're going to insert it into the template so that the same drop-down menu appears on every page, and that if you change the menu it will update on all the pages simultaneously.

You're going to start by removing the old menu on the pages.

9   With index.html page open, navigate to the sidebar and remove the menu from the sidebar area (just delete it, it's in the editable region).

10   Save the page and close it.

11   Repeat the same process for all the pages.

12   Open the template ecoLiving_template.dwt, and remove the same menu from the sidebar using the same technique.

13   Save the template and when prompted to update the changes, accept it to update all the pages created from the template.

14   Now you're going to remove the sidebar editable region to create a new one. Select the sidebar editable region by clicking on the cyan tab as shown on the screenshot below.

15 Choose **Modify > Templates > Remove Template Markup**.

16 Now place your cursor at the beginning of the sidebar code (use Code view or Split view) and insert the Spry menu bar by choosing **Insert > Spry > Spry Menu Bar**.

17 Set it to **Vertical** and press OK. When it appears on the page customise the menu elements as on the screenshots below.

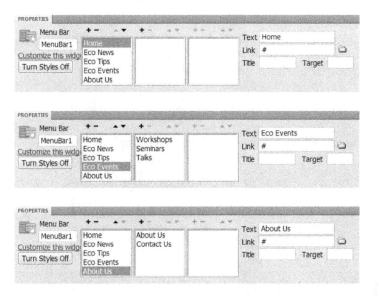

As you can see on the screenshot below, only the last two items: Eco Events and About Us have submenues.

18 Using the knowledge you have gained from the previous lesson where you inserted the Spry menu bar customise the menu so it matches the size of the sidebar and customise the colours for the menu elements so that the background is green and the text is yellow.

19 Change the colour of the text and the background on hover state to reversed colours.

20 Once you're customised the menu, add an editable region in the sidebar below the menu and call it **sidebar**.

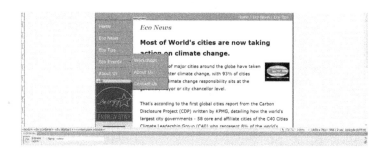

21 Save the template, update changes, and preview one of the pages in the web browser to make sure that the menu appears.

22 In the horizontal menu below the header remove the text Home | Eco News | Eco Tips. You don't need it anymore here.

23 If you haven't done it earlier, add links to the pages that exist within the Spry menu bar, i.e. **Home - index.html**, **Eco News - news.html**, **Eco Tips - tips.html** for now.

24 Finally, within the template, add some space directly under the drop-down menu by adding a line break as shown on the screenshot on the next page.

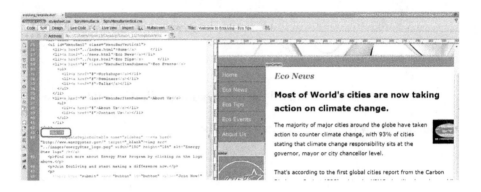

Congratulations, you have successfully updated the template with the Spry menu bar. You can close the template for now. Now you're going to insert the Spry accordion on one of the pages.

Spry accordion

Spry Accordion is a widget (a part of Dreamweaver, you will find it in the Insert panel, or under Insert menu), and it is a page element combining HTML, CSS, and JavaScript.

Spry Accordion is a set of panels that collapse with the content of one of the panels visible at one time. Thanks to that, you can store a lot of content in a small amount of space. The content in the accordion is revealed or hidden by clicking on the tab of the panel. The panels of the accordion expand and collapse in an animated fashion to reveal the content. The example on the next page shows the Accordion widget with one of the panels expanded:

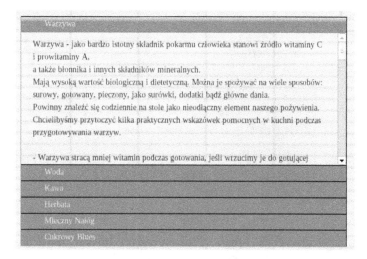

For a Spry Accordion to work you need two files (copied for you automatically by Dreamweaver, when you save and preview the page):

◦ SpryAccordion.js (JavaScript file),

◦ SpryAccordion.css (CSS file).

So, it is time to add the Spry Accordion to one of the pages.

25 Start by opening **news.html** if it's not already open. That's the page you're going to work with.

26 Insert the cursor into the heading **Most of World's cities...** and highlight it. Cut it to the clipboard (Ctrl+X on Windows, Cmd+X on Mac)

27 With your cursor blinking in the line, insert the Spry Accordion by clicking on Spry Accordion button in the Insert panel (Spry category).

305

Dreamweaver inserts the Spry Accordion widget. Initially there are two panels, so you're going to add another one. There are two parts in the accordion: tab area and content area. Tab area (with labels) will be titles for the articles that appear on the page. The body of the article will appear in the content area.

28 Select the text **Label 1** and paste the text you have just cut to the clipboard (Ctrl+V on Windows, Cmd+V on Mac).

29 Select the entire section for the first article (including the image on the right) and cut it to the clipboard the same way you did that with the title of the article.

30 Highlight the text Content 1 inside the panel and press Ctrl+V on Windows or Cmd+V on Mac to replace it with the text from the clipboard.

31 Save the page and you should see a dialogue box displaying files that Dreamweaver is going to copy into your site for the accordion to work properly. The screenshot on the next page shows the dialogue box.

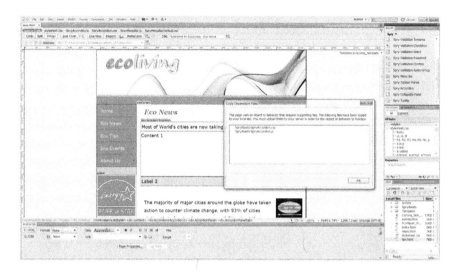

32. Just accept it and Dreamweaver will copy the files into the SpryAssets folder (if the folder doesn't exist, Dreamweaver will create it).

33. To add content for the second tab you need to have the Accordion selected. To do that, click on the cyan tab with the name **Spry Accordion: Accordion1** that appear when you rollover the top of the accordion. You should now see the properties for the Accordion display in the Properties panel.

34. Insert the cursor into the heading **Dutch study shows...** and highlight it. Cut it to the clipboard.

35. Select the text **Label 2** and paste the text you have just cut to the clipboard.

36. Select the entire section for the second article and cut it to the clipboard the same way you did that previously.

37 Highlight the text **Content 2** inside the panel and press Ctrl+V on Windows or Cmd+V on Mac to replace it with the text from the clipboard.

You have completed both panels and your page in the web browser should look like the page on the screenshot below:

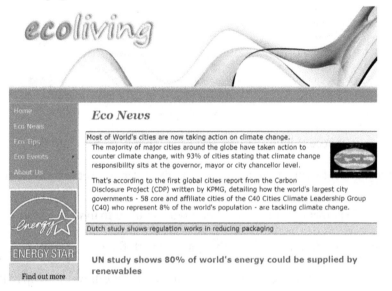

38 Now you can add additional panels (you need one more). To add or remove additional panels you use the Properties panel.

39 Select the cyan tab above the Accordion on the page. The Properties panel should now display the properties for the Accordion.

40 In the Properties panel click on Add Panel icon (+). A new panel is added to your Accordion.

41 Highlight the last heading on the page (the title of the article) and cut it to the clipboard.

42 Select the text **Label 3** and paste the text you have just cut to the clipboard.

43 Select the entire section for the last article and cut it to the clipboard the same way you did that previously.

44 Highlight the text **Content 3** inside the panel and press Ctrl+V on Windows or Cmd+V on Mac to replace it with the text from the clipboard.

45 Save the page and preview it in the web browser to test it.

You should now have an Accordion with three tabs and three sections / articles. Now you're going to customise the Accordion a bit with some CSS. Remember that the Accordion has its own stylesheet, so you're going to work with SpryAccordion.css.

Customising the Spry Accordion

Now you're going to customise the look of the Accordion so it matches the overall colour scheme of the website. You're going to start with the tabs.

46 Start by placing your cursor inside the first tab and inspect names in the tag inspector in the bottom left corner of the document window. The element customising the tab is the rule **.AccordionPanelTab**.

47 Navigate to the CSS Styles panel, find the **.AccordionPanelTab** rule and edit it.

48 Start by changing the background. Navigate to the Background category and set the options as shown on the screenshot below:

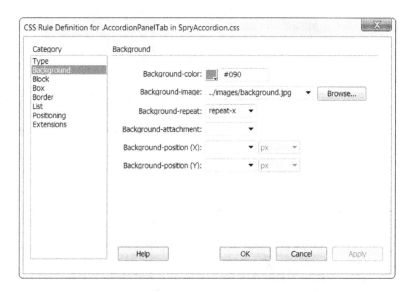

49 Navigate to the Type category and set the font colour to **#FF0** (yellow).

50 Still within the Type category, set the Font-size to **80%**.

51 Finally, in the Box category set Left Padding to **15px** (Same for all should be deselected). Press OK.

52 Save all the files and preview the page in the Live view. Test the Accordion. You will notice that when you roll over the tab, the text turns green. This doesn't look good so you're going to change that now.

53 Go back to the Design view and look for the rules that deal with the hover effect (in the SpryAccordion.css).

You will find two rules **.AccordionPanelTabHover** and **.AccordionPanelOpen .AccordionPanelTabHover**.

54   Change both rules so they have the same text colour - yellow and set the **Font-weight** to **Bold**, otherwise the hover effect would look the same as the original state of the tabs.

55   Now you're going to change the height of the panel. Find the **.AccordionPanelContent** rule and set the Height property to **300px**.

56   Finally, you're going to change the width of the Accordion. Find the **.Accordion** rule and set the **Width** to **90%** and give it **Left Margin 20px**.

57   Save all the files and preview the page in the Live view. Then close the page.

Spry tabbed panels

Spry tabbed panels are another example of a space-saving element or widget placed on a web page. It is a widget with a series of tabs at the top of the widget and when you click on one of the tabs, the content appears. In a Spry tabbed panel widget, only one panel opens at a time.

In this part of the lesson, you're going to add a Spry tabbed panel to EcoTips page.

58 Start by opening **tips.html**. Place your cursor at the beginning of the line that reads **Eco Living at home**.

59 Navigate to the Insert panel and choose **Spry Tabbed Panels**.

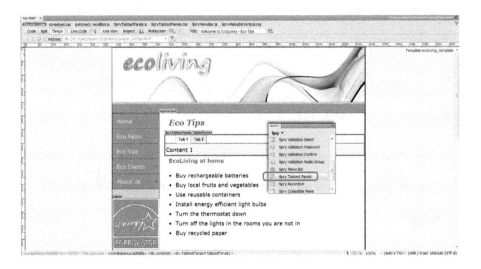

60 The Spry tabbed panels widget appears on the page with two tabs.

61 Highlight the first heading on the page **EcoLiving at home** and cut it to the clipboard.

62 Highlight the text in the first tab that reads **Tab 1** and replace it with the heading by pasting it (Ctrl+V on Windows, Cmd+V on Mac).

63 Now the first tab should read **EcoLiving at home**.

64 Repeat the steps for the second tab so that it reads **EcoLiving at work** instead of Tab 2.

65 Place your cursor over the first tab and when you see the eye icon, click on it to see the content for the panel - it should read **Content 1**.

66 Highlight the entire section for the first panel (the entire first list) and cut it to the clipboard.

67 Back in the panel, highlight the text that reads Content 1 and replace it with the list from the clipboard.

68 Repeat the steps for the second section.

69 Save all the files and preview the page in the web browser. When prompted to copy dependent files, click OK.

These are the files required by the Spry tabbed panel (as explained earlier at the beginning of the chapter, every Spry element requires some .js and .css files).

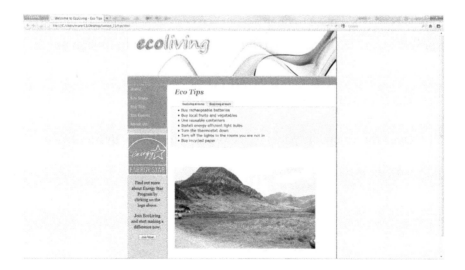

70 Test the panels and notice how the panel expands to fit all the content. Spry tabbed panels widget doesn't have width defined, it expands to fit the content.

71 If you want to customise the widget, edit **SpryTabbedPanels.css**.

72 If you want to add additional tabs, highlight the widget by clicking on the cyan tab that reads **Spry Tabbed Panels: TabbedPanels1** and use the plus sign (+) in the Properties panel to add any extra tabs.

Spry effects

Here's what you're going to do now. You're going to add one of the Spry effects to animate an image so that it fades in when the page loads. And you're going to achieve that without Flash as Spry effects use JavaScript, and you don't need to know any JavaScript for that! How great is that? To add Spry effects, you'll need to open a new panel called Behaviors because the Spry effects are basically JavaScript behaviours built into Dreamweaver.

73 Start by opening the home page - **index.html**.

74 Open the Behaviors panel by choosing **Window > Behaviors** as shown on the screenshot on the next page.

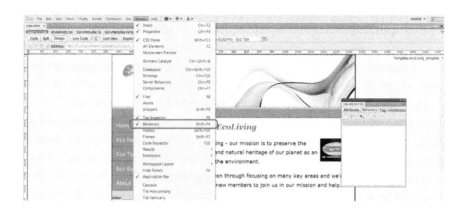

When the Behaviors panel opens, highlight the image on the right (the one slightly behind the Behaviors panel on the screenshot).

In the Behaviors panel click on the plus icon (+) and select **Effects > Appear/Fade**.

In the Appear/Fade dialogue box, set the following options:

- Target Element   - <Current Selection>
- Effect Duration   - 4000 milliseconds
- Effect   - Fade
- Fade from   - 0 %
- Fade to   - 100%

and click OK to accept the settings.

Test it in the Live view. As you click on the image, it fades in.

Looks great but it would be better if the image could fade in when the page loads instead of the user clicking on it. That's what you're going to change now

79 Exit the Live view and select the image on the page.

80 Navigate to the Behaviors panel and notice how the behavior is set up.

The behavior reacts to the onClick event. That's why the image only fades in when the user clicks on the image.

81 Click on **onClick** behavior to change it to **onLoad**.

82 Save and test the page in the Live view. When the page loads, the image will fade in in four seconds.

Congratulations! You have succesfully completed another lesson. Well done.

Review Questions

1. What are the three main Spry categories?

2. How do you add or remove panels in the Spry Accordion?

3. Do Spry elements require plug-ins?

4. Where will you find Spry effects?

Review Answers

1. There are three main Spry categories:
   ◦ Spry Effects, i.e. Slide, Fade
   ◦ Spry Widgets, i.e. Accordion, Tabbed panels
   ◦ Spry Data, using data to populate the page, i.e. XML.

2. To add or remove additional panels in the Spry Accordion you use the Properties panel.

3. No, when adding Spry elements to your pages, no plug-ins are required.

4. To add Spry effects, you'll need to open a panel called Behaviors

Lesson 12

Forms

In this lesson you're going to learn how to be more productive and how to:

- insert a Form

- insert text fields, radio buttons, check boxes

- insert drop-down menus

- insert buttons

- process form with PHP

This lesson will take about 1 hour 30 minutes to complete.

319

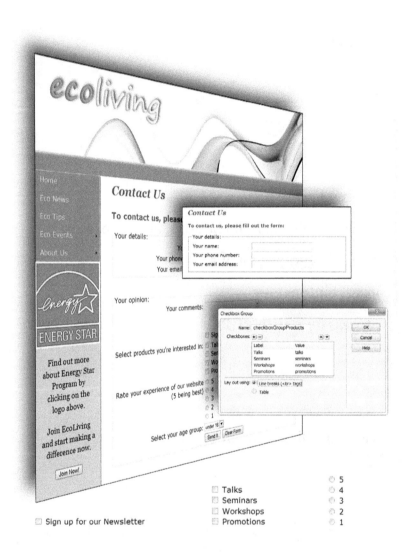

Online Forms

You may have come across the forms online before. Forms are interactive elements online that are usually used to gather some information from the visitors. It is like a form on paper, where you fill in some information about yourself, i.e. your details, comments etc. The form elements, fields, are used to gather the information from your visitors. Unlike with the paper forms, online forms can be easily changed/updated before the visitor sends it by simply resetting/clearing the form.

You can create a web form in Dreamweaver very easily by simply inserting form elements within the form element. The harder part is developing mechanism to handle the data when the visitor submits the form. Typically, web forms would be handled by web technologies like ColdFusion or PHP, and in this lesson you are going to use PHP to handle the form you are about to create.

There are a number of form elements and you are going to get to know them as you start inserting elements one by one. But first, you're going to create a new page and insert a form element.

1 Launch Adobe Dreamweaver CS5, if it is not already open.

2 If you see the Welcome Screen, click on Dreamweaver Site button to define a new Site. If you don't see the Welcome Screen (you may have disabled it through the Dreamweaver Properties), choose Site > New Site from the menu. The Site Setup dialogue box appears.

3 In the Site Name field, type **Lesson_12**.

4 In the Local Site Folder field, click on the folder icon to the right and navigate to the **Lesson_12** folder containing the files for this lesson.

5 Select **Lesson_12** folder, and click Open (Windows) or Choose (Mac). Then, click Select (Windows) or Choose (Mac) to choose this folder as your local root folder.

6 Click the arrow next to the **Advanced Settings** category on the left to reveal a list of tabs. Select **Local Info** category and next to **Default Images folder** field, click the folder icon. When the dialogue box opens, navigate to the images folder located inside Lesson_12 folder and click Select (Windows) or Choose (Mac).

7 In the Site Setup dialogue box click Save.

8 Choose File > New, and create a new page from a template.

The first step now is going to be to create a new page for the form (contact us page).

9 When the page opens, choose **File > Save as….**

10 Save As dialogue box appears. Save page as **contact.html**. Click Save.

11 Replace Eco News heading with Contact Us.

12 Highlight the entire content in the right column under the heading and delete it.

322

13 Under the heading type **To contact us, please fill out the form:** and change the formatting to **Heading 3**. Press Enter to move to the next line.

All the form elements need to be contained within the **form** element. You are going to insert the form element first. If you insert one of the fields outside the form element, the field will not be submitted with the form.

14 Navigate to the Insert panel and change the category to **Forms**.

15 Place your cursor under the subheading and in the Forms category in the Insert panel click on the Form icon to insert the form element.

Dreamweaver inserts the form element indicated by the red dashed line. As you are going to style the form a bit with some CSS, now you're going to give the form element its own unique ID.

16 Look into the Properties panel and you should find the **Form ID** in the top left corner. Type in **ecoLivingForm**.

17 Now give it **15px** margin on left and **30px** margin on right by creating a new CSS rule for **.content #ecoLivingForm**.

Text Form elements

Now it's time to start adding text form elements, i.e. text fields, text areas etc. Text fields are basic elements used to gather information from the visitors to your website. It is hard to imagine a form without any text form elements. You're going to start with text fields and then text areas.

Text fields are basically fields that accept letters and numbers and you can limit the number of character. But just before you insert the text field, you're going to insert a Fieldset first to create a logical group of form elements. After the Fieldset has been inserted, you're going to see a border around the elements that will go inside the Fieldset and the Fieldset also has a Legend that will display on the top.

18 Place your cursor inside the form element and insert a Fieldset from the Insert panel. When prompted for Legend, type **Your details:** and press OK.

19 Now inside the Fieldset you're going to insert the table and the first Text Field. Go to the Split view and find the code for the Legend.

20 Place your cursor after the closing tag for Legend, go back to Design view and insert a **Table**.

21 Set the Table to **3 rows**, **2 columns**, Table width **90%**, Border **0**, and Header **None**. Press OK.

22 Place the cursor in the first row in the right column and insert a Text Field For ID type **name**, for Label **Your name:**. Press **OK**.

NOTE: ID field will be used to process the form, hence no spaces and all lowercase. Label will appear on the page so you can use any characters you want.

23 Highlight the label on the page and drag it to the left column as shown on the screenshot below.

24 Repeat the process for the next row inserting another Text Field, but this time set ID to **phone** and Label to **Your phone number:**.

25 Once again drag and drop the label to the left column.

NOTE: When inserting a Text Field, leave Style set to Attach label tag using 'for' attribute, as this allows you to move the two elements and keep them linked together.

26 In the last row insert another Text Field for email setting ID to **email** and Label to **Your email address:**.

27 Drag and drop the label to the left column.

You're done with the first fieldset. Your page should now look like the screenshot below (this is the screenshot of the Live view).

Now, you're going to add another Fieldset for some comments and opinions of the visitors about the website and services.

28 Place your cursor before the closing tag for the first Fieldset (you may want to use Split view/Code view) and press Enter on the keyboard in Design view to add some space.

29 Insert another Fieldset and set the Legend to **Your opinion:**.

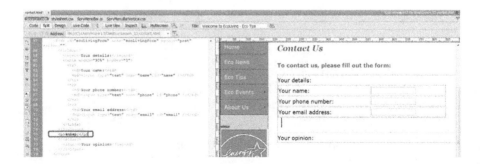

30 Now inside the Fieldset you're going to insert the table and the first Text Field. Go to the Split view and find the code for the Legend.

31 Place your cursor after the closing tag for Legend, go back to Design view and insert a **Table**.

32 Set the Table to **3 rows**, **2 columns**, Table width **90%**, Border **0**, and Header **None**. Press OK.

33 Place the cursor in the first row in the right column and insert a Text Area. For ID type **comments**, for Label **Your comments:**.

34 Highlight the label on the page and drag it to the left column.

Now that you have a few elements on the page you're going to customise these elements a bit.

35 Select the first Text Field (the box in the right column) and look into the Properties panel. It should display the properties of the Text Field. Set Char width to **25** - this will be the size of the box.

36 Set Max chars to **25** as well - this will be the maximum number of characters that can be entered into this box.

37 Repeat Steps 35-36 for phone number and email address text fields.

NOTE: Depending on the country you live in, you may want to limit the number of characters for the phone number, i.e. in the UK we have 11 digits.

38 Select the text area element in the second fieldset and notice that it's just a text field with multiple lines as defined in Num lines in the Properties panel. Set **Num lines** to **4** and **Char width** to **25**.

Now you're going to add another form element - a checkbox to let people sign up for our newsletter.

39 Place the cursor in the next row and insert a Checkbox. Set ID to **signup** and Label to **Sign up for our Newsletter**.

40 Select the Checkbox on the page and make sure that **Initial state** is set to **Unchecked** (in Properties panel).

Now you're going to do a bit more styling to the tables on the page. You're going to define widths of the columns and alignment of the form elements inside the columns. You're going to use CSS for that, of course.

41 Create new CSS rule in the Styles panel, set it to **Class** and call it **width300**. Set Width to **300px**, Text-align to **Right**, Vertical-align to **Top** and press OK.

42 Apply newly created class to both left columns.

Now you're going to add a Radio Group and a Checkbox Group. The main difference between the Checkbox Group and Radio Group is that with Radio Group the visitors will only be able to select one of the options, whereas with Checkbox Group they can select as many as they want. You are going to insert both elements.

43 Place the cursor in the next row, in the right column as usual and insert a Checkbox Group.

As with Text fields, Checkbox group has a number of IDs and Labels (in here called Label and Value, Label being the text displaying on the page and Value being the value being sent with the form).

44 Add data into the Checkbox Group as on the screenshot below.

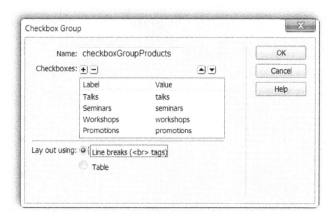

45 In the left column type **Select products you're interested in:**.

46 Save and test the page in either Live view or in a web browser.

47 What you may have now is a slight indent in the right column before the checkbox group. If you do, we'll fix it now.

48 If your page looks the same as mine, it looks like the checkbox group ended up being inside the paragraph, so your job will be now to remove the paragraph. You will do it manually in the code.

49 Go to the Split view (or Code view if you prefer) and find the code for the checkboxes. The code should start with this:

```
<td><p>

    <label>

      <input type="checkbox"
name="checkboxGroupProducts" value="talks"
id="checkboxGroupProducts_0" />

      Talks</label>
```

Notice the opening <p> tag in the code. That's what needs to be removed.

50 Find the opening p tag **<p>** and remove it.

51 Find the closing p tag **</p>** and remove it as well.

52 Save the changes and preview the page in a web browser. Everything should look fine now.

Now you're going to move on and insert a radio group on a page. The main difference between the checkbox group and the radio group is that with radio group only one of the options can be selected. You're going to use a radio group element to ask your visitor to rate their experience of the website.

53 Place your cursor in the last cell in the table and press the **Tab** key on your keyboard to add another row.

54 Press the Tab key once again to move the cursor to the right column.

55 In the right column insert a **Radio Group**.

56 In the **Radio Group** dialogue box change the name to **RadioGroupRating**. Set Labels and Values to 5, 4, 3, 2, and 1 as shown on the screenshot on the next page.

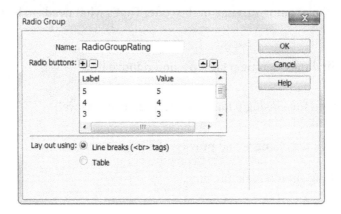

57 Press OK to insert the Radio Group.

58 In the left column type **Rate your experience of our website (5 being best)**.

59 If once again the group of buttons appears to be indented, repeat **Steps 50-51** to remove the <p> tag.

60 Save and preview the page.

61 Place your cursor in the last cell in the table and press the **Tab** key on your keyboard to add another row.

62 Press the Tab key once again to move the cursor to the right column.

Now you're going to add a drop-down menu to the form using Select (List/Menu) element from the Insert panel.

Select (List/Menu) element displays entries in a drop-down menu format. Where Lists differ from Menus is that with the Lists you can allow users to select multiple items instead of just a single one as is the case with the Menu.

To compare List and Menu to what you have learnt so far, Menu functions a bit like radio buttons - only one can be selected, whereas List works a bit like checkboxes.

In this part of the lesson, you're going to insert a menu element to ask your visitors about their age group.

63 Place your cursor in the right column in the last row of the table and insert Select (List/Menu) element using the Insert panel.

64 In the Input Tag Accessibility Attributes dialogue box type **ageGroup** in ID field, leave the Label field empty, and set Style to **No label tag**. Click OK.

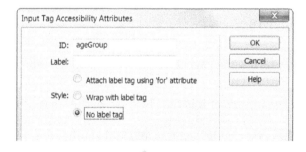

65 An empty menu appears on the page. Now you're going to add entries through the Properties panel. Highlight the element on the page.

66 Navigate to the Properties panel and click on List Values button.

67 In the List Values dialogue box add the Labels and Values as on the screenshot below.

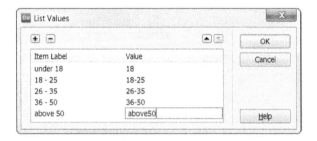

68 Click OK when done.

69 In the column next to the Menu type **Select your age group:**.

70 In the Properties panel you can choose what's going to initially display in the menu by highlighting it in the options next to **Initially Selected**. Highlight **under 18**.

71 Save and preview the page in the web browser. Test the form.

72 Back in Dreamweaver it is time to add a button that will submit the form. Place the cursor in the last row and add another one by pressing the **Tab** key on your keyboard.

73 Press the Tab key once again to move the cursor to the right column.

74 In the Insert panel click on Button icon to insert a button that will submit the form.

75 In the Input Tag Accessibility Attributes dialogue box type **submit** in the ID field. Set Style to **No label tag**. Click OK.

The Submit button appears at the bottom of the form and the Properties panel displays the properties of the button. Button's Value is set to Submit and that's what displays on the button on the page. You're going to change it now.

76 Change the Value field in the Properties panel to **Send It**.

You need another button here, one that resets the form so that a visitor could start over. You're going to insert it now.

77 Insert space after the Submit button and then repeat Steps 74-75 to insert another button, this time giving it an ID of **reset**.

78 Change the Value field in the Properties panel to **Clear Form**.

79 Set the Action in the Properties panel to **Reset form**.

80 Save the page, you're almost done.

Now it's time to make the form work. On the next page you're going to specify the action for the form to be processed.

Processing the Form

You have inserted all necessary elements into the form, now it is time to specify how the form is going to be processed. A typical example, and easy to accomplish, would be to send the form data by email and that's what you're going to do now.

By now you may be thinking about typing mailto command into the Action field (with the entire form selected).

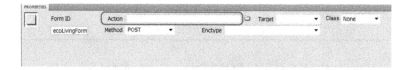

However, you need to keep in mind that many people won't have email clients installed on the machines they use to access your website, so you're going to use PHP to process the form and have it sent by email to you. And the visitor won't even know that! Pretty clever.

In Lesson 12 folder I've included a file **sendresults.php** for you. You're going to use it in this exercise. This is the file that is going to process the form and send it by email.

81 Highlight the entire form and in the Properties panel (as shown on the screenshot above) you should see the Action field. Next to it, you'll find a folder icon.

82 Click on the folder icon and in the **Select File** dialogue box select **sendresults.php**. Click OK.

Now you're going to edit the **sendresults.php** for form processing. There are only a few things to change, so don't be scared. You can do it even if you have no experience in programming.

83   Save and close contact.html.

84   Open **sendresults.php**. If you're in Design view, you won't see anything on a page. Switch to Code view.

I tried to make this as easy as possible. There are only four lines of code that need to changed, actually just three near the top of the page.

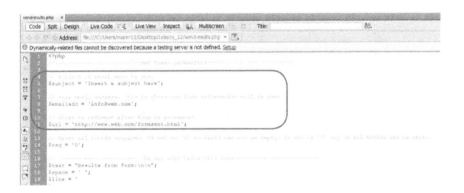

85   To make this work, you'd need to upload your website to the server, so I'll just tell you what you would need to change. You would set:

◦ *subject* to the subject of the email that will be sent to you,
◦ *email* to the email address where the email would be sent (NOTE: email needs to be on the same server as the website),
◦ *url* to the address of the page that would open after the form is processed (usually a "Thank you" page).

86 To finish the lesson you can create a "Thank you" page and point the PHP file to the page, so it opens when the visitor clicks Submit button.

87 Since you are not uploading the website to the server in this lesson, when the "Thank you" page was created, change the Action for the form to this page.

88 Save the page and preview it.

Congratulations! You have successfully completed the final lesson. Well done.

Review Questions

1. How important is the form element in processing the form (what's going to happen if you insert one of the fields outside the form element)?

2. When inserting a Text Field, why would you want to set Style to Attach label tag using 'for' attribute?

3. When inserting form elements, what are the differences between ID and Label?

4. What is the difference between Checkbox Group and Radio Group?

Review Answers

1. If you insert one of the fields outside the form element, the field will not be submitted with the form.

2. When inserting a Text Field, leave Style set to Attach label tag using 'for' attribute, as this allows you to move the two elements and keep them linked together.

3. ID field will be used to process the form, hence no spaces and all lowercase. Label will appear on the page so you can use any characters you want.

4. The difference between the Checkbox Group and Radio Group is that with Radio Group the visitors will only be able to select one of the options, with Checkbox Group they can select as many as they want.

Lesson 13

Publish your website

In this lesson you're going to publish your website to the internet and:

- define a remote site

- upload files to the server

This lesson will take about 30 minutes to complete.

Define a remote site

When working in Dreamweaver, you will be working with two sites as you work on live websites. One of them is a *local site* - this is a local version of the website on your computer. Another one is a *remote site* - this is a remote/live version of the website on server, server being another computer connected to the internet.

To connect to the server, Dreamweaver allows you to use one of the many methods:

◦ **FTP** - File Transfer Protocol - this is the most popular, standard method for connecting to the web server.

◦ **SFTP** - Secure File Transfer Protocol - this is a newer method for connecting in a more secure manner.

◦ **Local/Network** - this is usually used when the web pages are first uploaded to a local server, and then upload to the web server online. This kind of connection can be used to use a testing server without uploading files to the web.

◦ **RDS** - Remote Development Services - this was developed by Adobe for ColdFusion and is used to work with ColdFusion websites.

◦ **WebDav** - Web Distributed Authoring and Versioning - this is a web based system known as Web Folders or iDisk.

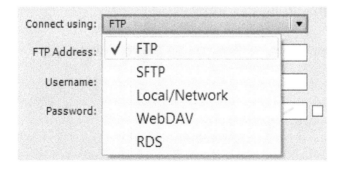

343

1 Launch Adobe Dreamweaver CS5, if it is not already open.

2 If you see the Welcome Screen, click on Dreamweaver Site button to define a new Site. If you don't see the Welcome Screen (you may have disabled it through the Dreamweaver Properties), choose Site > New Site from the menu. The Site Setup dialogue box appears.

3 In the Site Name field, type **Lesson_13**.

4 In the Local Site Folder field, click on the folder icon to the right and navigate to the **Lesson_13** folder containing the files for this lesson.

5 Select **Lesson_13** folder, and click Open (Windows) or Choose (Mac). Then, click Select (Windows) or Choose (Mac) to choose this folder as your local root folder.

6 Click the arrow next to the **Advanced Settings** category on the left to reveal a list of tabs. Select **Local Info** category and next to **Default Images folder** field, click the folder icon. When the dialogue box opens, navigate to the images folder located inside Lesson_13 folder and click Select (Windows) or Choose (Mac).

7 In the Site Setup dialogue box click **Servers** category.

8 Click the Add New Server icon and in the Server Name field type **Eco Living server**.

9 From the **Connect using** drop-down menu choose FTP.

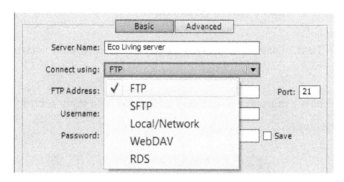

10 In the FTP Address field type the URL of your FTP server.

If you use a hosting provider, most of us do, you will be provided with an FTP address. Enter the address as it was provided to you. Sometimes it may be something like: ftp.ecoliving.org with the name of your site. Check with your hosting provider.

11 In the Username field type your FTP username.

12 In the Password field type your FTP password.

Make sure you type the username and password exactly as they were provided to you as these are often case-sensitive.

13 In the Root directory field, type the name of the folder that contains your website - all the files that are made public on the web.

14 If you don't want to type your password every time you try to connect to the server, check **Save** option on the right.

15 Click **Test** to see if Dreamweaver can connect to your server.

If Dreamweaver manages to connect successfully to your server you should see this message:

16 Click OK to close the dialogue box.

17 Click Save to save all the server settings.

18 Click Save once again to save all the site settings and exit the Site Definition dialogue box.

19 You may see the dialogue box informing you that the cache will be recreated because of the change in the settings.

20 If you see the cache message, just click OK to build the cache.

Congratulations! You have successfully established a connection to your remote server.

Uploading your site

Now it is time for you to upload the files to the remote server to put them online. When you transfer files from your local site to remote site, you're putting files in Dreamweaver terms. Dreamweaver will put files into the equivalent folder on your remote site.

What's great about Dreamweaver is that you can upload one file as easily as the entire website in one session. When uploading the website to the remote site, Dreamweaver may ask you if you want to upload the dependant files - these will be files like images, CSS, scripting files, flash content etc.

21. Go to the Files panel and click the Expand icon to activate Expanded panel mode.

In the Expanded panel mode you will see the Files panel take over your entire screen and there will be two main columns: one for local site (**Local Files**) and one for remote site (**Remote Server**) as shown on the screenshot on the next page.

347

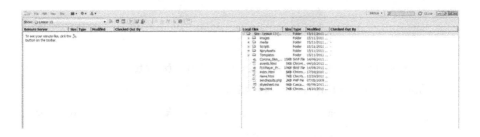

22 To connect to your server you need to click on Connects to Remote Host icon.

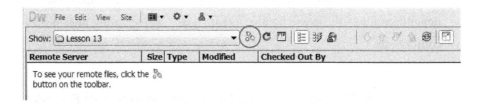

23 Click Connects to Remote Host icon and in just a moment you should be connected to your web server.

24 You can now start uploading the files. Select one of the files in your site and click the Put icon.

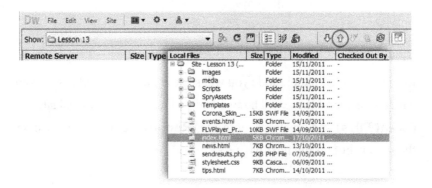

25 Dreamweaver will prompt you if you want to upload the dependent files as explained a bit earlier.

26 Time for uploading the entire website. Select the site folder, right-click on it and from the context menu choose Put.

27 A dialogue box will appear asking you to confirm that you want to upload all the files within a website. Click OK.

Dreamweaver is now uploading all the files within your local site to the remote site (to the web server). Depending on how many files you have it may take just a few seconds or maybe a minute (or longer).

28 When Dreamweaver is finished uploading the files, open your web browser and test the website by typing the URL - such as http://eco-living.org.

Congratulations! You have designed and built an entire website and successfully uploaded your website to the web server. Well done!
Now you are ready to put your knowledge to practise and start creating websites for others.

Index

www.ingramcontent.com/pod-product-compliance
Lightning Source LLC
Chambersburg PA
CBHW080151060326
40689CB00018B/3933